P9-DHD-809

SYSTEMATIC PROBLEM-SOLVING AND DECISION-MAKING

Sandy Pokras

CRISP PUBLICATIONS, INC.
Los Altos, California

SYSTEMATIC PROBLEM-SOLVING AND DECISION-MAKING

Sandy Pokras

> *The message from the moon . . . is that no problem need be considered insolvable.*
>
> —Norman Cousins

CREDITS
Editors: **Michael G. Crisp and Francine Lundy Ruvolo**
Designer: **Carol Harris**
Typesetting: **Interface Studio**
Cover Design: **Carol Harris**
Artwork: **Ralph Mapson**

Copyright © 1989 by The Viability Group, Inc.
Printed in the United States of America

Crisp books are distributed in Canada by Reid Publishing, Ltd., P.O. Box 7267, Oakville, Ontario, Canada L6J 6L6.

In Australia by Career Builders, P.O. Box 1051 Springwood, Brisbane, Queensland, Australia 4127.

And in New Zealand by Career Builders, P.O. Box 571, Manurewa, New Zealand.

Library of Congress Catalog Card Number 88-72260
Pokras, Sandy
Systematic Problem-Solving And Decision-Making
ISBN 0-931961-63-7

ABOUT THIS BOOK

SYSTEMATIC PROBLEM-SOLVING AND DECISION-MAKING is not like most books. It stands out from other self-help books in an important way. It's not a book to read—it's a book to *use.* The unique "self-paced" format of this book and ample worksheets, encourage the reader to get involved and try some new ideas immediately.

Using the simple yet sound techniques presented will help a reader to define, analyze, understand and solve problems. Also, readers will learn to sharpen their decision-making abilities.

This book (and other titles listed in the back of this book) can be used effectively in a number of ways. Here are some possibilities:

—Individual Study. Because the book is self-instructional, all that is needed is a quiet place, some time and a pencil. By completing the activities and exercises, a reader should not only receive valuable feedback, but also practical steps for self-improvement.

—Workshops and Seminars. The book is ideal for assigned reading prior to a workshop or seminar. With the basics in hand, the quality of the participation will improve, and more time can be spent on concept extensions and applications during the program. The book is also effective when it is distributed at the beginning of a session, and participants "work through" the contents.

—Remote Location Training. Books can be sent to those not able to attend "home office" training sessions.

There are several other possibilities that depend on the objective, program or ideas of the user.

One thing for sure, even after it has been read, this book will be looked at—and thought about—again and again.

ABOUT THE AUTHOR

Sandy Pokras is President of The Viability Group, Inc. a company that specializes in communication training, organization development, and learning processes. Sandy has been active in management training and consulting since 1973 and holds a certificate in Interpersonal Counseling from the Advance Organization of Copenhagen. He has authored a number of training guides and videotapes that deliver his uniquely workable formula to build people skills in a pragmatic way.

For more information about The Viability Group, write P.O. Box 2216, Castro Valley, California 94546 or call (415) 727-1772.

CONTENTS

PART I—Introduction 1
Personal Expectations Worksheet 3
Your Objectives 4
Personal Learning Contract 5

PART II—Process Overview 6
What Is A Problem Anyway? 7
Problem Characteristics Checklist 8
Consumer Tech Case Problem 10
Problem Solving Method Overview 12
Problem Solving/Decision-Making Outline 13
Overview Checklist 14

PART III—Communication Dynamics 15
Communication Dynamics 16
How To Get Agreement On Problems 17
What Makes Meetings Work? 18
Meeting Roles 19
Discussion Leader Skills Checklist 20
Group Problem-Solving Questionnaire 23
Meeting Evaluation Form 24
The Six Step Problem-Solving/Decision Making Process 26

PART IV—Problem Recognition 27
Step One: Problem Recognition. 28
Problem Recognition Techniques 30
Data Collection Worksheet 33
Sample Target Data 34
Questions To Uncover Problems 36
Brainstorming Guidelines 38

PART V—Problem Labelling 40
Step Two: Problem Labelling 41
How To Find A Problem Label 43
Sample Label Comments 45
Label Worksheet 46
Force Field Analysis: A Versus B 48
Force Field Analysis: Obstacles 49
Key Word Analysis Worksheet 51
Problem Label Test 52

TABLE OF CONTENTS (Continued)

PART VI—Problem Analysis...53
Step Three: Problem Cause Analysis 54
Cause-Effect Analysis Exercise 59
How To Find The Root Cause 60
Six Techniques To Identify Problem Causes 61
How To Know When You've Found The Root Cause Of A Problem 67
Root Cause Analysis Program Checklist 68

PART VII—Optional Solutions.........................69
Step Four: Optional Solutions 70
Optional Solutions Worksheet 73
Positive/Negative Forces Analysis 75

PART VIII—Decision-Making 76
Step Five: Decision-Making 77
How To Make A Decision 78
Consequences Worksheet 80
Prioritizing Methods Checklist 82
Standards And Criteria List 84
Criteria Matrix 85
Decision Test 88

PART IX—Action Plan 89
Step Six: Action Plan 90
The Value Of Action Planning 91
Action Item Worksheet 93
Action Planning Question Checklist 94
Action Plan Form 95
Monitoring Techniques 96
Contingency Planning Worksheet 97
How To Handle Resistance To Change 98
Final Action Plan Test 100

PART X—Summary 101
Evaluation Of Objectives 102
Personal Summary 103

PART I INTRODUCTION TO SYSTEMATIC PROBLEM-SOLVING AND DECISION-MAKING

Have you heard the old cliché *"there are no problems, only opportunities?"* This might sound like pie-in-the-sky optimism to anyone stuck in the middle of a difficult puzzle or a stressful people problem. But by using the proven, logical problem-solving and decision-making system presented in this book you can create opportunities from problems.

This book will show you how to rationally confront problems and systematically resolve crises. The decision-making method you learn will help you break down touchy situations into component parts which can easily be dealt with individually. By using the comprehensive system presented, you'll know how to define, unravel, analyze, and solve tough dilemmas and recurring foul-ups.

This book's primary emphasis is on communication in business. But the entire method presented here can be applied to personal situations as well.

The biggest problem-solving mistake is dealing with the symptoms of a problem rather than its "root causes." Sometimes even the "experts" don't find the fundamental reason the problem exists right away. When symptoms are treated, "band-aid" decisions are made. Then old symptoms reappear, or new ones emerge, and the same old problem returns.

Step-by-Step Method

By taking the steps of systematic problem solving and decision-making you can prevent problems from recurring. They include...

> **STEP 1: PROBLEM RECOGNITION**
>
> **STEP 2: PROBLEM LABELING**
>
> **STEP 3: PROBLEM-CAUSE ANALYSIS**
>
> **STEP 4: OPTIONAL SOLUTIONS**
>
> **STEP 5: DECISION-MAKING**
>
> **STEP 6: ACTION PLANNING**

THE BENEFITS AND SKILLS

What will be the advantages when you follow the step-by-step method presented on page one? Those who apply the techniques of *Systematic Problem-Solving and Decision-Making* will receive the following benefits and learn the following skills:

BENEFITS AND SKILLS

☐ Definitions   You will learn to accurately define the real problem to avoid solving symptoms.

☐ Solutions   You can implement once-and-for all solutions instead of temporary band-aid fixes.

☐ Decisions   The decisions you make will be good decisions that can be implemented and that will stick.

☐ Meetings   Your meetings will reflect productive problem-solving and decision-making.

☐ Buy-in   You will learn to obtain buy-in from conflicting viewpoints to help define problems, reach decisions, clarify solutions and implement action plans.

☐ Teamwork   You will enjoy effective teamwork between differing individuals and groups while solving problems.

YOUR EXPECTATIONS

To get the most out of this book, you need to relate what you read to your personal situation. Answering the following questions can help you to focus on your typical problems and decision situations.

PERSONAL EXPECTATIONS WORKSHEET

Write your answers below:

What problem situations would you like to correct?

What difficult decisions do you need to work through logically?

Which recurring problems and decisions would you like to resolve once and for all?

Which of your problem-solving and decision-making skills would you like to improve?

Select a specific situation from the above to use as your Personal Case Problem while working through this book.

> As you work through this book, refer back to this worksheet. Experience has shown that this is the best way to learn a self-development method like this.

YOUR OBJECTIVES

Rate your interest in the following objectives.

I want to: **OBJECTIVES RATING**	Top Priority	Interested	Some Interest	Little Interest
1) understand the *steps* of this problem-solving system.	☐	☐	☐	☐
2) know how to use the analytical *techniques* in each step.	☐	☐	☐	☐
3) recognize the vital role *communication* plays at each step.	☐	☐	☐	☐
4) know what *questions* to use in order to stimulate communication at each step.	☐	☐	☐	☐
5) understand the *anatomy* of problems and why they persist.	☐	☐	☐	☐
6) understand how to confront problems to *prevent future stress.*	☐	☐	☐	☐
7) know how to distinguish between the *causes and effects* of problems.	☐	☐	☐	☐
8) know how to *label* a problem to facilitate discussion and analysis.	☐	☐	☐	☐
9) know how to find a problem's *root cause.*	☐	☐	☐	☐
10) know how to brainstorm optional *solutions.*	☐	☐	☐	☐
11) know how to evaluate optional solutions to *decide* on the most workable strategy.	☐	☐	☐	☐
12) understand the importance of *action planning* to implement the chosen solution.	☐	☐	☐	☐
13) know how to *apply* the system to real-life problems as they occur in the future.	☐	☐	☐	☐

YOUR COMMITMENT

You've now had a chance to clarify your expectations and objectives. Your next step is to make an active commitment. The *Personal Learning Contract* below presents the essential items. Take an affirmative step and check each item to which you will commit. Then sign your name as an affirmation of your commitment.

PERSONAL LEARNING CONTRACT

Check
Your
Commitment

I plan to be more logical, analytical, and systematic in solving problems and making decisions. _____

I want to take steps to insure I find the "real problem" before beginning to solve it. _____

I'm willing to involve others affected by the problem in the solution process in order to promote support and teamwork. _____

I'm willing to work through the exercises in this book, do my best to relate them to the problem to be solved and then implement my solutions. _____

I will manage my time so I can concentrate on learning the skills presented in this book by studying them without distraction or interruption. _____

I intend to use what I learn and consciously put it into practice. _____

Agreement:
I want to receive the maximum benefit from this program by carrying out this learning contract.

_____   _____
(signature)   (date)

PART II
PROCESS OVERVIEW

WHAT IS A PROBLEM ANYWAY?

DEFINING TERMS

What does the term *problem* mean? Since the word problem is used so often in this book, you need a crystal-clear understanding of the word. What do you think ''problem'' means? Write your immediate thoughts below:

Your Definition Of The Term *Problem:*

PROBLEM CHARACTERISTICS

The following checklist summarizes the characteristics of problems. Items on this list always seem to be true about problems. It might be said that if these items exist, then your situation qualifies as a true problem. Check which of these characteristics apply to the cases you identified on the *Personal Expectations Worksheet* on page 3.

Problem Characteristics Checklist

Characteristics	These apply to my situations
Incomplete communication: conversations have broken down or haven't even been started so that full understanding is lacking.	☐
Unknowns: information is missing.	☐
Inaccurate information: some of the known information is wrong.	☐
Confusion: people involved find themselves in a mental fog, stressed, or overwhelmed by stimuli and choices.	☐
Hidden emotions: emerging feelings tend to come out as you examine the situation.	☐
Different viewpoints: you and others have conflicting ideas.	☐
Changing impressions: as you investigate the situation, ideas, feelings, and explanations change, sometimes radically.	☐
Balanced dilemma: a tug of war exists where no one person or idea is able to win.	☐
Persistence: the situation won't disappear.	☐

PROBLEM ANATOMY

A problem is basically a dilemma with no apparent way out; an undesirable situation without a solution; or a question that you can't currently answer. It's not just that things are different from the way you'd ideally like them to be—it's that you can't <u>fix</u> them no matter what you do. It's not simply a question you haven't yet answered—it's one you can't explain no matter what you do. And it's a conflict or crisis that keeps coming back no matter what you do about it.

The anatomy of a problem boils down to this simple picture:

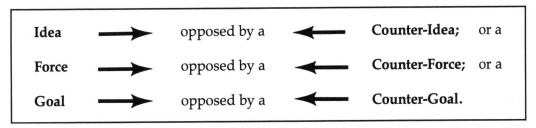

In words, a problem is an...

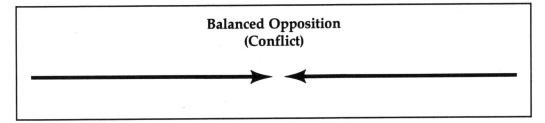

This table could go on but I'm sure you get the idea. For example:

you want to go shopping	but	**you also want to save money,**
you have to work with J.R.	but	**you can't stand the person,**
your department thinks everything is working fine	but	**your quality inspector wants some changes.**

The balanced opposition of situations is what generates the stress and confusion. The balance makes the problem persist. If one side gets stronger and wins the struggle, the problem disappears. For example, your boss comes into the picture and decides how to handle things and everyone goes along with the decision. Poof, no more indecision. (Of course, if the underlying forces aren't resolved by this arbitrary choice, the problem will reappear.)

CASE PROBLEM

To make the techniques presented in this book more realistic, consider the situation in the *Consumer Tech Case Problem.* Throughout the book we will apply the methods presented to this problem.

Consumer Tech Case Problem

Consumer Tech is a small company which develops and sells consumer products based on new technology. They have an extremely successful product, the Automatic Toothbrush. Recently, the Engineering Department came up with a dramatic new improvement. They've perfected a hands-free circuit which allows the brush to brush teeth electronically. Its called the Electronic Toothbrush.

This has created a problem. The Engineering Manager wants to introduce the development right away. Unfortunately, during test production runs, the Manufacturing Manager has encountered problems producing the new components. The Quality Manager is helping to determine what's causing the problems.

The Marketing Manager wants to announce the improvements immediately, but the Finance Manager is worried about making the large inventory of Automatic Toothbrushes obsolete if the introduction is done too quickly.

Formal meetings about the Electronic Toothbrush, led by the company President, quickly deteriorate into heated arguments which lead nowhere. And impromptu water-cooler meetings in the hall often become shouting matches.

Looking at the *Problem Characteristics Checklist* on page 8, you will find all the problem characteristics present in this situation. Consumer Tech has tried to find a solution, but things are not progressing. It's becoming increasingly clear that some balanced opposition exists that no one has yet recognized. Unless this conflict is uncovered and resolved, things will probably go from bad to worse.

CASE PROBLEM—YOUR RESPONSE

If you wanted to help, what would you do? Write your thoughts below. Feel free to refer to anything you have read thus far in this book. Later, after you have completed the book, revisit this page to see how your suggestions have changed.

I would help Consumer Tech by:

PROBLEM-SOLVING METHODOLOGY

The ideal method of resolving problems and making difficult decisions involves two steps. This magic formula is guaranteed to work: in fact, it's never failed when applied correctly. Here it is:

> **I. Define the problem.**
>
> **II. Decide how to solve it.**

You already knew that, right? Although it seems obvious, most problem-solvers and decision-makers don't do a very good job of Phase I, Problem Definition. Instead, they rush off to Phase II, Solution Decision. Unless you define the problem thoroughly and accurately, your solution may not address what's really wrong underneath. In fact, most students of this system report that finding solutions is relatively easy. The difficulty is knowing exactly what to analyze and resolve.

How do you define a problem? And how do you find the best solution? Take a look at the *Problem-Solving/Decision-Making Outline* presented on the facing page. This summarizes the process, and will be referred to as the PS/DM Outline throughout the book. Let's see how it works.

"BEFORE I STATE THE PROBLEM, ARE THERE ANY SOLUTIONS?"

PROBLEM-SOLVING/DECISION-MAKING OUTLINE

Each step below has a specific result. Only when you reach that result should you go on to the next step. For the best results don't skip <u>any</u> step.

PROBLEM DEFINTION PROCESS	RESULT
1. Recognition Discuss and document individual views, proven facts, and relevant symptoms, until everyone involved accepts that there is a problem.	**Agreement that an issue needs resolution.**
2. Label Clearly document both sides of the exact conflict you want to resolve.	**An agreed-upon statement of the problem.**
3. Analysis Find and agree on the <u>single</u> most fundamental source of the problem.	**Unanimous identification of the root cause which needs correcting.**

SOLUTION DECISION-MAKING PROCESS	RESULT
4. Options List <u>all</u> alternative strategies that have the slightest chance of resolving the problem and its root cause.	**A complete list of possible solutions.**
5. Decision-Making Choose the best solution on your list by objectively evaluating the optional strategies.	**A firm joint decision on the chosen solution.**
6. Action Plan Organize systematic steps of tasks, timing, staff, and resources to implement the decision in the real world.	**A complete step-by-step road map to translate the decision to reality.**

Each step of this outline will be discussed in detail throughout the balance of this book. Before going into each step in detail, it helps to have some guidelines to follow while applying the PS/DM Outline. The *Overview Checklist* presented on the next page sums up the best way to approach any problem/decision situation.

OVERVIEW CHECKLIST

Review the checklist below to evaluate how well you currently deal with problems and decisions. You can refer back to it whenever you want to check your status.

PROCESS OVERVIEW CHECKLIST

Check those things you do currently when making a decision or solving a problem:

I plan an agenda directed to a specific result. _____

I stay on track and follow the agenda I've planned. _____

I set and stick to ground rules for participation. _____

I break down big problems into "bite-sized" chunks. _____

I complete each step before moving to the next. _____

I return to the previous step if progress bogs down. _____

I know which technique I'm using at each point. _____

I trust the process and keep on it as long as it works. _____

I don't mix methods from different processes. _____

I include all people or units affected. _____

I openly consider divergent ideas as valuable input. _____

I accept and integrate all views and feelings. _____

I write down all thoughts, suggestions, and input. _____

I keep a public running record of group discussion. _____

I keep all material visible to all group members. _____

I know which questions to ask at each step. _____

I draw out complete answers from all present. _____

I discipline myself to listen and respond. _____

I assign distinct roles in the meeting. _____

I stimulate the group's synergy and creativity. _____

I seek agreement between divergent positions. _____

PART III
COMMUNICATION DYNAMICS

COMMUNICATION DYNAMICS

Before starting the six step process outlined on page 13, do you know what determines whether or not a problem-solver or decision-maker can make the process work? If you answered communication skills, you are right.

Poor communication causes barriers to solutions, while good communication skills are strong catalysts to problem-solving. Poor communication is an indication of the existence of a problem and may, in fact, be the cause of the trouble.

This part presents some critical mechanics to make communication work during the Problem-Solving and Decision-Making process.

GETTING AGREEMENT

Without mutual agreement that a problem exists, it can't be discussed, analyzed or solved effectively. Good problem-solvers and decision-makers achieve agreement by applying this vital awareness: other viewpoints must be sought after, respected and accepted. Communication is the process to make all this work.

How To Get Agreement On Problems, shown on the facing page, summarizes *Guidelines* for making the logical process work with human beings who sometimes aren't so logical. *How To Apply It* defines how to implement each guideline.

HOW TO GET AGREEMENT ON PROBLEMS

GUIDELINE	HOW TO APPLY IT
If you feel you have a problem with someone or something, then there **definitely is** a problem.	Don't ignore it or let yourself be talked out of it. Probe for the other's awareness of the problem.
If a problem exists, everyone is **aware** of it in some way. Remember that your **awareness** of a problem may be quite different from others.	To find out another's awareness of a problem, ask how things are different from the way they should be, or simply ask what their awareness of the problem is.
Find an accepted or observable fact as a **reference** point to start with.	Use production statistics, specific events, confirmed facts, something the other person has said, but <u>no</u> value judgments.
Find where **viewpoints** overlap.	Analyze the information you receive from everyone and see what's in common.
Ask before you dictate.	State the general area you want to talk about, but immediately ask for the other person's feelings, thoughts, or observations.
Solicit the other person's **point of view.**	Don't enforce your viewpoint on them, but show empathy for their position until they accept yours.
Avoid a **threatening,** accusative climate.	Don't use leading or judgmental questions (*''Are you still screwing up?''*) or lectures that elicit guilt or impose value judgments.
Create a strong and open working **relationship.**	If you're confronted with severe defensiveness or intimidation, use a less threatening approach.
Discover the falsehoods and **unknowns** that are causing the problem to persist.	Keep communicating until you find them.

WHAT MAKES MEETINGS WORK?

Let's apply guidelines from **How to Get Agreement on Problems** to meetings. Think back to several recent group problem-solving or decision-making situations you were involved in. What made the meetings work and what got in the way?

To answer this question, use the following **Force-Field Analysis** worksheet: *Positive/Negative Forces For Meetings.* You will find this format several times later in this book. Two columns are headed by opposing brainstorming questions, in this case dealing with meetings. The question on the left asks for positive forces and the question on the right asks for negative forces. By playing a plus against a minus, your thinking loosens up and differences stand out more clearly.

When you fill in this form, don't use general terms like *''communication''* but specific descriptions like *''Joe wasn't prepared''* and *''Jerry knew what questions to ask.''*

FORCE-FIELD ANALYSIS WORKSHEET:
POSITIVE/NEGATIVE FORCES FOR MEETINGS

What makes meetings productive and effective?	What makes meetings unproductive and ineffective?

MEETING ROLES

Experts find that meetings work best when roles are well-defined. The *Meeting Roles* chart below explains how to separate responsibilities for meeting participants. The *Discussion Leader* or traffic cop and the *Recorder* or public note-taker are neutral. Everyone should either be a *Participant* or a *Presenter*.

Those present can wear different hats. Keeping roles separate is critical.

The most significant factor, the *Authority Figure* of the group (i.e. the boss), must relinquish roles to meeting participants. If the authority figure doesn't do this, contributors will hold back, edit what they say, or challenge authority. An effective meeting will produce an open climate, a free exchange, and creative thinking without undue concern about the boss's reaction. This is hard to achieve, but defining roles will help.

MEETING ROLES

Discussion Leader
Directs the traffic of the discussion: announces each topic and its time frame, calls for input, asks stimulating questions, balances participation, reminds wanderers of the issue, and summarizes at the end. Remains neutral and doesn't pass judgment without permission from the group.
Recorder
Keeps an accurate, public, running record of what is said. Writes key words clearly on a flip chart or blackboard so that speakers feel they were heard correctly. Doesn't try to document everything but just gets the main points down.
Presenter
Presents outside information and major viewpoints in a systematic fashion. Articulates the position, gives supporting evidence, involves listeners, leads their thought process, and responds to questions.
Participant
Speaks their mind fully and clearly, listens intently, and absorbs what others have to say.
Authority Figure
Ideally, the senior manager of the group should play an equal role in creative meetings. Since this is difficult in practice, it is recommended that the authority figure only assume the role of ''special participant,'' the one with the final say. Since bosses are expected to be decisive, making one the discussion leader (who is supposed to be neutral), usually distorts a free and open exchange.

THE DISCUSSION LEADER

The most challenging role is that of *Discussion Leader* who directs the participation, but doesn't evaluate what is said.

Controlling a dialogue has three phases: 1) starting—getting individual or group discussions going, 2) guiding—steering the dialog once started, and 3) stopping—summarizing, wrapping up, or getting people to stop when they've already finished. These sub-skills are detailed in the following ***Discussion Leader Skills Checklist.*** Use this checklist to assess the effectiveness of a discussion leader and to identify those sub-skills needing development.

DISCUSSION LEADER SKILLS CHECKLIST

Starting Skills

_____ Know the issues before beginning.

_____ Have easy reference notes and outlines available.

_____ Get attention and call people to order.

_____ Announce agenda items.

_____ State points and problems clearly.

_____ Establish realistic time frames.

_____ Ask questions to get the group thinking.

_____ Call all people by name.

_____ Draw people out, especially quiet ones.

_____ Notice and call on those with something to say.

_____ Introduce new viewpoints into an ongoing discussion.

Guiding Skills

_____ Listen carefully to all participants.

_____ Use silence effectively and wait out pauses.

_____ Read indicators and body language.

_____ Remain neutral to insure acceptance of all ideas.

_____ Be sensitive and adjust to moods to keep things moving.

_____ Follow the agenda and keep discussions on track.

_____ Restate topic to focus the group on one issue at a time.

_____ Steer discussions toward the desired results.

DISCUSSION LEADER SKILLS CHECKLIST (Continued)

Guiding Skills (Continued)

_____ Clarify meanings and restate questions.

_____ Avoid interfering with interactions.

_____ Turn provocative questions back to the group.

_____ Balance participation between different styles.

_____ Mediate conflicting viewpoints so all are heard.

_____ Manage diversions, digressions and distractions.

_____ Watch the clock and keep time-frames apparent.

_____ Reflect on repeating patterns and asking for reaction.

Stopping Skills

_____ Acknowledge what people have said.

_____ Insure each participant gets to finish.

_____ Prevent individuals from talking at the wrong time.

_____ Stop people who say things over and over.

_____ Protect individuals by discouraging attackers.

_____ Let long-winded dominators know they've been heard.

_____ Check that questioners receive satisfactory answers.

_____ Announce when time deadlines are approaching.

_____ Summarize what has been accomplished.

_____ Know when to recap by listening for common themes.

_____ Show consensus by noticing and announcing it.

_____ Ask for decisions and suggest conclusions.

DOCUMENTATION DURING MEETINGS

Effective problem-solvers and decision-makers keep accurate, up-to-date, legible notes. In group settings, this trait is especially important. The real pay-off of good paperwork habits comes during later phases of the PS/DM Outline.

Because of the confusion factor, especially at the beginning of a problem-solving situation, all sorts of information will be mixed together. Why go over this again later? If you carefully document items **as you go along,** you'll come to a decision sooner than those who do a poor job of recording the process.

Benefits of Documentation

The following statements are benefits of clear documentation:

- Provides clearer, more accurate communication   _____
- Formally acknowledges individual contributions   _____
- Remembers and saves information for future use   _____
- Provides a fixed reference point for later use   _____
- Provides a history for all time   _____
- Allows outsiders to familiarize themselves with situation   _____
- Shows evidence of the analysis process used   _____
- Encourages equal participation in a group   _____

Helpful Techniques for Documentation

Following are some techniques that may help make your documentation easier. Check any you plan to use:

- ☐ Tape pages or butcher paper sheets on walls or windows and keep notes on them.
- ☐ Record what is said and decided on flip charts.
- ☐ Use brief statements and short words that convey the meaning.
- ☐ Have the group itself draft documents, rotating the chore.
- ☐ Tape record brainstorming meetings and have them transcribed.
- ☐ Have a trusted stenographer present to take notes.

EVALUATE YOUR NEXT MEETING

The next time you're in an interactive meeting, try this experiment to bring focus to the individual roles. After the process, have each member answer the questions on the *Group Problem-Solving Questionnaire.* Then discuss each participant's reactions with the group. The objective is to discover how communication works best in this setting. Either you will find that each individual has naturally gravitated toward adopting a specific role, or you need to define your meeting responsibilities better.

GROUP PROBLEM-SOLVING QUESTIONNAIRE

1. How was the agenda chosen?
2. Who led the discussion? Why?
3. Did you record issues presented?
4. Did all attendees participate? If no, why not?
5. Was a consensus reached? If no, why not?

THE BOTTOM LINE

Next time you are part of a problem-solving or decision-making meeting complete the following form to help you zero in on the points that were well handled and those that could be improved.

MEETING EVALUATION FORM

CRITERIA	0 to 10 RATING (10 = High)

Preparation

1. Participants informed ahead of time. _____

2. Participants fully prepared for their role and contribution. _____

3. Participants committed to dealing with common issues. _____

4. Comfortable, uninterrupted, set-up room. _____

5. Started on time. _____

6. Clear well-presented agenda.

Organization

7. Agenda followed efficiently with flexibility. _____

8. Focused on one issue at a time. _____

9. All viewpoints of each issue fully considered before moving on. _____

10. Smooth dialogue occurred through coordinated interchange of speaking and listening roles. _____

11. Good pace maintained reflecting group momentum. _____

CRITERIA	0 to 10 RATING (10 = High)

Participation

12. Participants actively contributed to a balanced interchange. _____

13. Participants clearly presented their genuine ideas and feelings. _____

14. Participants listened attentively to others' contributions. _____

15. Participants responded directly and constructively to others' input. _____

16. Spontaneous combustion of creative energy and thought stimulated full disclosure. _____

Climate

17. Spirit and emotional level of group was high. _____

18. Discussion dealt with issues and their solution, not personalities and their conflicts. _____

19. Individuals accepted others' viewpoints without personal attack or non-verbal put-downs. _____

20. Members supported the leader and recorder as they guided the group. _____

21. Disruptions and interruptions were smoothly disposed of. _____

Closure

22. Final judgements suspended until all input tapped. _____

23. Succinct summaries recapped progress and acknowledged results. _____

24. Discussion steered effectively to consensus and then stopped. _____

25. Action items clearly announced and documented. _____

26. Follow-up monitoring mechanism established. _____

27. Meeting ended on positive feeling and mutual understanding. _____

THE SIX STEP PROBLEM-SOLVING AND DECISION MAKING PROCESS

The next several parts of this book cover a systematic method of problem-solving and decision-making. Following is a list of the steps you will cover:

STEP 1: RECOGNIZING THE PROBLEM

STEP 2: LABELLING THE PROBLEM

STEP 3: ANALYZING THE CAUSE OF THE PROBLEM

STEP 4: EXPLORING OPTIONAL SOLUTIONS TO THE PROBLEM

STEP 5: MAKING A DECISION TO SOLVE THE PROBLEM

STEP 6: CREATING AND FOLLOWING AN ACTION PLAN TO RESOLVE THE PROBLEM

PART IV
STEP 1:
PROBLEM RECOGNITION

STEP 1: PROBLEM RECOGNITION

Problem-solving and decision-making begins by recognizing that a situation needs resolution. Sometimes a problem gradually builds without being noticed until it surprises you. Even when the trouble is obvious, it is a good idea to start with Step 1.

Problem Recognition examines the ''tip of the iceberg.''

THE ICEBERG OR 80/20 RULE

No matter how large the tip of an iceberg seems, 80% of it lies below the surface of the water.

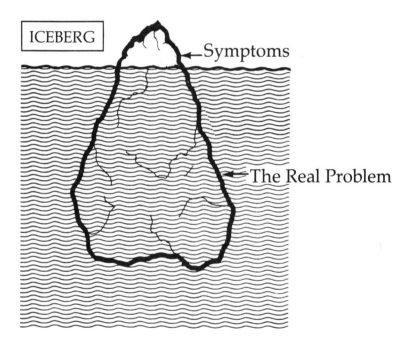

It is the same way with problems. No matter how serious or stressful the first encounter with a problem may seem, it is only a symptom of the underlying trouble or real problem.

Symptoms may be trivial, like one minor defect, or they may be serious issues that must be dealt with quickly, such as falling production levels. Regardless, they are simply side effects of the real problem that lies beneath the surface.

The Iceberg Rule reminds you to have patience. You've got to understand the whole problem before rushing off to solve it. So examining, researching, investigating, tabulating and studying are the watchwords of Step 1.

OPENING DISCUSSION—
A GOOD PLACE TO START

Problem recognition often starts with a discussion to gather symptoms from those involved. An iceberg may look different when viewed from different angles. Open-minded listening and genuine empathy are required to objectively assess other viewpoints. The objective is to get as much related information as possible ''on the table.''

During an opening discussion your impressions of the problem may change. What may seem like a technical problem (such as not being able to find the bug in the computer software program) may turn out to be a personality conflict between programmers who don't share information with each other. Studying the human factors (soft symptoms) involved is important to really understand the problem. These include: feelings, divergent opinions, frustrations, personal reactions and hearsay. These are not hard scientific data (hard symptoms), but valuable nonetheless. During the opening discussion you should discover all of the problem's effects and consequences, both hard and soft symptoms, and uncover all initial viewpoints of the situation.

Once listed it's helpful to categorize viewpoints as **hard** or **soft.**

Hard Data	**Soft Data**
Facts, results, events, history, statistics, forces, goals, procedures, physical phenomena, observable deviations, time factors, trends, productivity, quality and performance levels.	Feelings, opinions, human factors, frictions, attitudes, satisfaction levels, stresses, frustrations, personality conflicts, behaviors, hearsay, intuition, ''gut'' reactions, mental blocks.

HOW MUCH IS TOO MUCH?

How far do you take Problem Recognition? You could say that getting all the facts (hard) and feelings (soft) is your target. The trouble is to know when you've discovered them all. (Actually, you will continue collecting facts and uncovering impressions throughout all the steps of the PS/DM process.)

A general guideline that you've completed Step 1 is when everyone agrees that a problem needs resolution, and when all initial perceptions have been heard, listed and categorized.

PROBLEM RECOGNITION TECHNIQUES

> There are four techniques in Step 1 that will help you recognize a problem:
>
> **1. Symptom Identification**
> **2. Research Methods**
> **3. Data Collection Interviews**
> **4. Group Brainstorming**

Certain techniques may be more appropriate in some cases than others. Watch for the need to vent frustrations. Problems and decisions are stressful and people involved may need to release their emotional reactions. Venting is not always fun for the listener. However, when the air is cleared, people often become more rational and cooperative.

Each technique will be examined individually:

1. Symptom Identification: The *Symptom List* is a simple form used to tabulate all visible manifestations, consequences, and effects. It is compiled by discussing and listing the initial data and perceptions of everyone involved.

Following is an example of a Symptom List filled in with some of the facts from the Consumer Tech Case Problem on page 10.

Symptom	Hard	Soft
Current product selling well	✔	
New product dramatic new improvement	✔	
Engineering wants to make change now		✔
Production department has component problems	✔	
Poor quality likely based on test results	✔	
Marketing Manager ready to announce new product		✔
Finance Manager worried because inventory levels high	✔	✔
Meetings lead nowhere		✔
Heated arguments		✔

Search for both hard and soft data. They're not always distributed 50-50, but you must examine both sides.

The following may be used for your *Personal Case Problem*.

SYMPTOM LIST

Symptom	Hard	Soft

PROBLEM RECOGNITION TECHNIQUES (Continued)

2. Research Methods: The *Data Collection Process* will help you systematically study the background and effects of the problem. This ten-step method leads you through designing and conducting an investigation of the problem. The *Data Collection Worksheet* on the facing page includes a series of methods you may choose for your study. A sheet outlining **Sample Target Data** is shown on page 36.

DATA COLLECTION PROCESS

1. Identify the overall kind of information needed in order to define the problem. (Use the *Data Collection Worksheet*).

2. Select the data collection methods best suited for this type of information.

3. Define the specific target data you hope to collect with each appropriate technique (See *Sample Target Data*).

4. Collect the data required.

5. Analyze the data for patterns.

6. Establish a method to confirm the analysis, such as an experiment or more focused data collection process.

7. Collect data to confirm the pattern.

8. Document data and analysis in understandable form.

9. Prepare a visually-oriented presentation if others need to use your analysis.

10. Present your data and analysis.

DATA COLLECTION WORKSHEET

To be successful, first identify what target data you're after, and then design your research to focus in that direction.

General Information Needed To Define The Problem:

Data Collection Method

Survey Questionnaires

One-on-One Interviews

Production Statistics

Quality Statistics

Financial Statistics

Work Sampling

Technical Experiments

Time/Motion Studies

Checksheets

Focus Groups

Other:

Specific Target Data

SAMPLE TARGET DATA

Results

Production levels _____
Quality levels _____
Error and rework levels _____
Customer satisfaction _____
Performance against target _____
Expenditures versus budget _____
Profit margin _____
Return on investment _____

Resources

Personnel and training _____
Time _____
Capital _____
Production capacity _____
Physical space _____
Equipment _____
Inventory _____

Organization

Structure and function _____
Roles and responsibilities _____
Personnel policies and procedures _____
Management performance _____
Strategic planning system _____
Organizational communication system _____
Management information reporting system _____
Management style and corporate culture _____
Staff morale _____

External Environment

Other departments _____
Vendors _____
Labor _____
Economy/industry _____
New technology _____
Marketplace _____
Job market _____
Educational institutions _____
Political _____
Competitors _____
Public goodwill _____

Obligations

Stockholders _____
Contractual agreements _____
Legal restrictions _____
Labor contracts and laws _____
Government regulation _____
Environmental considerations _____
Social responsibility _____
Financial commitments _____
Employee health and welfare _____

PROBLEM RECOGNITION
TECHNIQUES (CONTINUED)

3. Data Collection Interviews: Typically the individual or group that starts the PS/DM Outline in motion doesn't have all of the related data. The research process can become extensive. Many problem-solvers and decision-makers use one-on-one interviews or group meetings as an initial data-gathering tool.

Data collection interviews are results-oriented, discussions specifically designed to understand an individual's view of the problem. The interviewer poses questions, listens, and takes notes, but does not talk much. It is critical to know what needs to be asked before the interview.

The checklist, *Questions To Uncover Problems* on the next page, suggests some appropriate queries. This list can be used as a data collection planning aid. When trying to discover a problem that someone hasn't been completely up front about or, dealing with a group that doesn't really understand the situation, check off those questions that you think will get you the information you need.

One word of caution: interviews can be inefficient or unproductive unless carefully structured in advance. Individual meetings are time-consuming. And voluminous notes take time to analyze. However, face-to-face meetings generate the most reliable information so they need to be seriously considered.

DATA COLLECTION INTERVIEW

QUESTIONS TO UNCOVER PROBLEMS

Check those you plan to use during your case problem:

—————— How are things going?

—————— What problems have you had lately?

—————— You seem (troubled/upset/worried) lately. What's happening?

—————— What do you feel has been different around here lately?

—————— What do you think changed?

—————— How has your work been going?

—————— Where do you need help?

—————— What are you satisfied or dissatisfied about?

—————— What do you find confusing?

—————— What is your position on this matter?

—————— What's on your mind?

—————— Lately I've noticed some indications of (lateness/slower work/lower quality). What do you think?

—————— You don't seem yourself these days. How come?

—————— What are your feelings about this (conflict/situation)?

—————— What opinions do you have about this problem?

—————— What (tensions/problems/disagreements/misunderstandings/conflicts/troubles) have you been aware of lately?

—————— What is your evaluation of this situation?

—————— How closely do you think we've been seeing eye to eye lately?

—————— Where do you think our views differ?

—————— What have I done that you (disagree with/object to/dislike/disapprove of/not understand/are confused about)?

—————— What about your (viewpoint/attitude) do you feel I've missed?

—————— What do you think are our chances of success on this program?

—————— What ideas and suggestions do you have regarding this project?

—————— In what areas do you feel (confident/a lack of confidence)?

—————— What's bugging you?

—————— What's happening?

—————— What's wrong?

—————— Who is involved and how?

—————— How do you see what's going on?

—————— How does the problem impact you?

PROBLEM RECOGNITION
TECHNIQUES (Continued)

4. **Group Brainstorming:** Getting a group of involved parties together for brainstorming has some obvious time management advantages. Brainstorming is typically a creative discussion where people build on each other's contributions to produce a comprehensive picture of the situation. Like the interview format, planning is required to make it work. Brainstorming must be led and managed effectively to keep the conversation focused.

The question ''What do we know about this problem?'' (or possibly others from the list *Questions To Uncover Problems)* provides the right focal point for group brainstorming as a data collection tool. Done right, you can help create tremendous creative leaps through joint energy.

AN UNPRODUCTIVE BRAINSTORMING SESSION

BRAINSTORMING GUIDELINES

Following are some helpful guidelines to apply to your brainstorming sessions. The discussion leader's role takes on added importance if this method is to be successful. If participants edit, judge, react negatively, or just frown at another's contributions, brainstorming breaks down.

BRAINSTORMING GUIDELINES

Question	1	The discussion leader clearly announces the focus of the session—the key question the group will be answering.
Post	2	The recorder writes down this key question.
Toss Out	3	All participants toss out as many ideas as possible.
Accept	4	All ideas, however impractical or crazy, are accepted.
Record	5	The recorder posts all ideas for everyone to see.
Prompt	6	The discussion leader keeps posing the key question without variation to keep the process on track.
No Editing	7	The discussion leader reminds the participants, as necessary, that no one is allowed to edit, criticize or evaluate any suggestion overtly or covertly until the process is done.
Build	8	Participants build on others' ideas. This triggers new thoughts which snowball the group process.
Synergy	9	By focusing this interaction, the group taps the creative energy of each participant and fuses it in a chain reaction—This is synergy, a combined or cooperative action which is more productive than the sum total of all individual efforts.

BRAINSTORMING GUIDELINES
(Continued)

Use the Brainstorming Guidelines and evaluate your success with the following Brainstorming Checklist.

BRAINSTORMING CHECKLIST

Guideline	Yes/No
1. Was the question clearly presented and posted for all to see?	_____
2. Were participants drawn out by noticing their body language and attitudes?	_____
3. Were participants questioned and coaxed only as needed?	_____
4. Was all input acknowledged?	_____
5. Was everyone encouraged to participate equally?	_____
6. Did the recorder write down all new contributions?	_____
7. Did the group help the recorder capture key ideas accurately?	_____
8. Did the process stay on track?	_____
9. Were ideas constructively built on by other contributions?	_____
10. Were new points of view proposed if the creative flow lagged?	_____
11. Did the discussion leader and recorder remain neutral without evaluating or steering the discussion to their own views?	_____
12. Were the ground rules of brainstorming reinforced by immediately policing any editing, criticism, or evaluation?	_____
13. Did the group stay stimulated and energized?	_____
14. Was any consensus recognized and summed up when it occurred?	_____

PART V
STEP 2:
PROBLEM LABELLING

STEP 2: PROBLEM LABELLING

After completing Step 1, you should have a wealth of data on your problem. It may be confusing and you still may not know what kind of a problem you have. Group participants may have different interpretations of the same issue.

After a problem recognition session on our Consumer Tech example, some labeled it a manufacturing problem. Others called it a marketing problem. Still others felt it was a petty personality conflict. A management analyst looking from the outside would label it a planning problem. Each reaction has some validity.

A problem will look different from different vantage points. Those doing the looking may label it with different words even though they're talking about the same issue. Whether differences of opinions are about details or major issues, disagreement blocks the necessary teamwork to resolve things.

THE ICEBERG RULE AGAIN

This difference of viewpoint can be called *The Lifeboat Corollary* of the Iceberg Rule. (A corollary is a secondary rule derived from a major principle.)

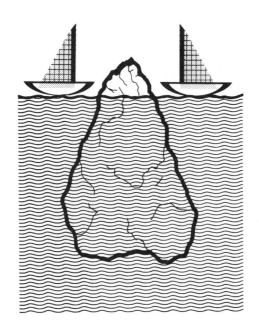

People in each lifeboat view the obstacle that sunk their ocean liner from a different angle. *The Lifeboat Corollary* says when this occurs, it is not possible to agree on descriptions. A common example is a manager who says an employee has a negative attitude. Does the employee buy that? Not usually. In fact, the result is usually that the worker feels the boss is the one with a distorted outlook.

WHAT IS A PROBLEM LABEL?

Step 2 attempts to identify and label both sides of the conflict in a way that everyone can accept. The label can be a phrase that highlights the key issue or the major obstacle. It should describe how things are affected, what needs to change, and the scope of the problem.

For example, everyone in the Consumer Tech situation would agree there was: *Disagreement on how to proceed with the new product feature. One group wanted to introduce the new feature now and the other wanted a more methodical implementation plan.*

The result of Problem Labelling is a simple agreed-upon statement of the common denominators of the problem. You need to identify the central issue that needs resolution. This should give you a unifying statement of the main problem.

WHY BOTHER?

Why go to the trouble of generating a label? A label functions as a **clearcut reference point** to focus on during the solution and decision-making process.

The label is like the flag shown below that every lifeboat can see from any direction. The dotted arrow indicates that the function of the label is to lead to the hidden reaches of the iceberg (or problem to be solved).

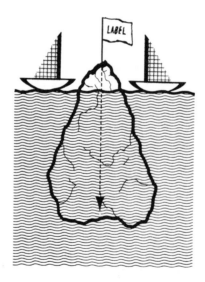

More importantly, all viewpoints must agree on what is to be solved. Outward dissension or internal disagreement at this point will destroy any chance for the logical analysis in Step 3. If those involved can answer *"Yes, that's the problem"* to a label, then they <u>own</u> their part of the problem. They'll be involved from the inside and really want to help solve the problem.

HOW TO FIND A PROBLEM LABEL

There are four techniques that will help you find a label for a problem:

1. Data Analysis
2. Brainstorming
3. Force Field Analysis
4. Key Word Analysis

Let's take a closer look at each:

1. Data Analysis: The most straightforward way to find a workable label is to sift through the symptoms looking for a common denominator. The *Data Analysis Worksheet* helps you think this through. Here's how you use it:

Fill in key **symptoms** in the left column. Search for patterns. Examine symptoms to identify recurring factors. Categorize symptoms in related groups to identify the **type** of problem at hand. Examples of types are: technical, work habits, interpersonal, organizational, personnel, hardware, political, schedule, financial, service, efficiency, communication, etc. Look for common **denominators** until the central issue is clear.

DATA ANALYSIS WORKSHEET

Symptom	Type	Denominators
Common Denominators/Patterns:		

HOW TO FIND A PROBLEM LABEL (CONTINUED)

2. **Brainstorming:** Use a *Label Worksheet* to list possible statements of the problem. One popular question used in brainstorming is: *"How are things different from the way we want them to be?"* Other possible target questions are:

> *"What is the problem?"*
>
> *"What is the central issue?"*
>
> *"How does the existing situation differ from the ideal scene?"*
>
> *"What do you want to cure or eliminate?"*
>
> *"What type of problem are you involved in?"*
>
> *"What conflict of ideas or intentions are you involved in?"*

Be sure you define both sides of the conflict. One way to accomplish this is to define what specific situation you would like to change and what the obstacle is to this change. *"Record breaking temperatures during August"* isn't a problem until you add *"are killing our garden."* If the second side of the problem was *"are killing elderly citizens who can't afford air conditioning,"* you can see how a label would shift the focus.

The *Sample Label Worksheet* gives actual examples of labels developed in Problem Solving workshops.

SAMPLE LABEL COMMENTS FROM ACTUAL PROBLEM-SOLVING WORKSHOPS

We can't meet the fixed inflexible customer ship date for documentation of new software due to continuing engineering changes right up to the last minute.

Lack of communication at shift turnover prevents the next shift from knowing how to handle unresolved problems quickly.

I have a new job and need direction to be successful, but my manager rates me low and doesn't help me improve.

A new software program doesn't meet the specifications and can't be fixed in time to meet the announced one-month release date.

I need to work with a coworker, but we can't stand each other.

An accounting program is needed for regular timely invoices, but no matter what's done to fix it, the program keeps bombing.

I keep getting more work assignments than can be handled at once in a quality way, but all of them are assigned ''number one priority'' with a due date of ''as soon as'' possible.

We need to fix a customer's problem on the phone but he/she is too emotional to give the facts.

A Label Worksheet is provided on the next page for your use.

46

LABEL WORKSHEET

HOW TO FIND A
PROBLEM LABEL (Continued)

3. Force-Field Analysis: A two-column Force-Field Analysis process helps to identify a label for a problem. Two suggested applications are presented, an *A versus B* format and an *Obstacles* format.

The *A versus B* format, generates a label which defines two conflicting forces. For example,

> *"we should introduce the new product feature right away versus we should proceed carefully until we handle manufacturing and inventory concerns."*

The *Obstacles* format lets you list what you want or what you need and then what prevents you from getting it. For example,

> *"we want to introduce the new product feature right away, but quality problems prevent this from being a great idea."*

FOUR TECHNIQUES FOR LABELLING A PROBLEM

FORCE-FIELD ANALYSIS:
A Versus B

What do you want?	What don't you want?

FORCE-FIELD ANALYSIS:
OBSTACLES

How do you want things to be? What do you need?	What obstacles prevent you from getting it?

HOW TO FIND A
PROBLEM LABEL (Continued)

4. Key Word Analysis: Key Word Analysis is a method of defining pivotal or disputed words or concepts. Communication is critical to effective problem-solving and decision-making. Sometimes semantics becomes a barrier. Semantic problems occur when different people have different meanings for the same key words. Using the *Key Word Analysis Worksheet* on the next page will clarify disputed words and terms to help come up with clearer and more acceptable labels.

To conduct a Key Word Analysis:

1) Select the word/term that seems to be the hang-up.
2) Write it in the top box of the worksheet.
3) Have the group define this key word specifically in as many ways as possible.
4) Select one meaning everyone agrees on and include that definition in your label, or replace the offending word in your original label with a more acceptable word.

In the Consumer Tech case, *quality* is an interesting word to define. Here are the initial reactions from members of the staff.

SAMPLE KEY-WORD ANALYSIS WORKSHEET

Keyword	Quality	
Definition		
Engineering Manager	⟶	Acceptable rejects (usually 5% or less)
Quality Manager	⟶	Zero defects
Marketing Manager	⟶	''Best'' on the market
Finance Manager	⟶	Product with the highest profit margin
President	⟶	Product which makes the stock price soar

Key-Word Analysis is only a supporting technique that provides problem-solvers and decision-makers with a valuable troubleshooting tool.

KEY-WORD
ANALYSIS WORKSHEET

Key Word

Define the key word as specifically as possible in as many ways as you can:

TEST YOUR WORK

Regardless of which method you use to arrive at a label, it's a good idea to test its effectiveness before proceeding. The *Problem Label Test* summarizes what makes an effective label. Run down the list, evaluate your proposed label, and adjust it accordingly. Experience has shown that inadequate labelling is one of the biggest reasons for poor problem definition.

PROBLEM LABEL TEST

Does the label...	<u>Yes</u>	<u>No</u>
Define what you want to solve?	☐	☐
State generally what aspect of the problem you want to cure?	☐	☐
Explain precisely what you want to change?	☐	☐
Identify both sides of the conflict?	☐	☐
Define what the obstacle is to what goal?	☐	☐
State the central, key issue?	☐	☐
Clearly and specifically document the dilemma?	☐	☐
Define the type of problem you're dealing with?	☐	☐
Generate agreement from all sides of the conflict?	☐	☐
Identify the ownership of the problem (who HAS it)?	☐	☐

PART VI
STEP 3:
PROBLEM-CAUSE ANALYSIS

STEP 3:
THE PROBLEM-CAUSE ANALYSIS

Problem-Cause Analysis produces the true problem definition. So why have we taken valuable time with Steps 1 and 2? Because it is extremely difficult to sort through the mental and emotional issues that cloud a problem. Previous steps helped create general awareness of what the problem is and isn't. These steps helped sort out the **causes,** contributing forces or stimuli that raised the problem in the first place from the **effects**, the symptoms, and by-products of the causes.

Step 3 looks for the <u>root cause</u> of the problem. The root cause is a controllable, solvable force which explains why the problem exists. Chester Barnard, an early author on the process of management, called this "the limiting factor." As chief executive of a large regional telephone company several decades ago, he found that the only problems which reached his desk were ones with a missing link. When he was able to ferret out this missing link or "limiting factor," a problem could finally be resolved once and for all.

THAT ICEBERG AGAIN

A dentist once pointed out that the term **root cause** doesn't fit the image of *The Iceberg Rule*. Well, maybe so, but the picture still demonstrates that we're searching for the basic core of the iceberg.

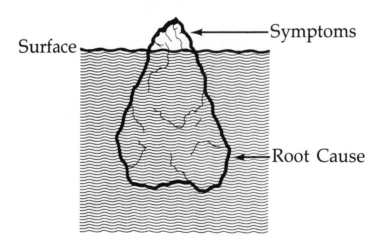

During Step 3, you will identify contributing forces that make the problem worse, sort through partial explanations that are possible causes, and weed out the by-product effects. You might think you've found the answer too soon. As you analyze your answers, the layers beneath the surface show that often partial explanations are found for why the problem exists. The **root cause** is at the bottom. It's the pivotal reason that started the problem in the first place and must be dealt with in order to find a long-term workable solution.

A SPECIFIC EXAMPLE

The layers beneath the surface of the iceberg illustrate a significant feature of the anatomy of problems. Typically, people try to fix the superficial symptoms or partial explanations which stem from the root cause.

FOR EXAMPLE: a worker hears a rumor from an inside source about plant closings and assumes the worst—*"I'm going to lose my job."* Even though it isn't true, it creates insecurity, so the worker puts out feelers for a new job. A supervisor hears about it and starts giving the "cold shoulder" treatment to the seemingly disloyal employee. If job offers fall through, the worker is now stuck with bad working conditions.

The employee may not understand this compounding sequence or be able to communicate with the supervisor about the foolish assumption that was made. Or, the worker may feel the need to protect an inside source.

The layers look like this, with the latest symptoms on top and the more fundamental causes below. To follow the timeline, read from the bottom up:

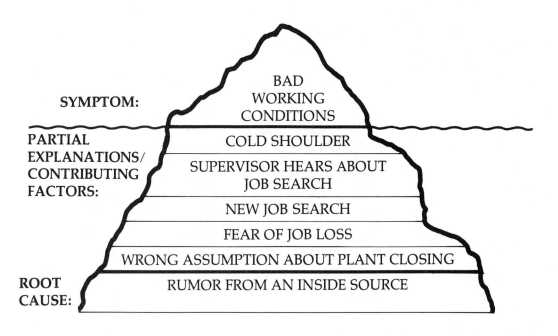

SYMPTOM:
BAD
WORKING
CONDITIONS

PARTIAL
EXPLANATIONS/
CONTRIBUTING
FACTORS:

COLD SHOULDER

SUPERVISOR HEARS ABOUT
JOB SEARCH

NEW JOB SEARCH

FEAR OF JOB LOSS

WRONG ASSUMPTION ABOUT PLANT CLOSING

ROOT
CAUSE:

RUMOR FROM AN INSIDE SOURCE

If this snowballing series of events was openly examined it could be cleared up. A little temporary embarrassment might remain but no permanent damage would be done.

YOU CAN HANDLE IT

Sometimes Problem-Cause Analysis yields a root cause that seems unsolvable. This factor can't be the actual root cause because it's not a controllable force that can be dealt with.

Some years ago an insurance branch office ran into severe cash problems early in the spring. The causes were traced back to a snowstorm at the corporate headquarters some weeks earlier. During the extreme winter weather, no one could get to work and the mail stopped for several days.

Was the weather the root cause? Absolutely not. It was a partial explanation, but why would bad weather, not uncommon at that time of year, suddenly cripple the branch? The Problem-Cause Analysis showed cash wasn't managed properly to prepare for this worst case scenario that winter. The root cause was because the branch controller was recuperating from surgery without a replacement. Until someone took the financial reins (and maybe a new policy prevented unfilled key employee positions in the future), more financial problems would result.

REMOVE THE KEY

The root cause explains why a problem persists, reappears, and repeatedly draws people into stress, frustration, and confusion. It's like a keystone—the one brick that holds the arch together.

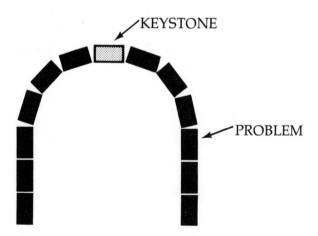

Find the keystone, remove it with a good solution, and the problem will collapse.

When those involved have an uplifting *"Aha!"* experience that fully explains the situation, you've found the root cause. "Aha" is a term for the moment of recognition and realization. Often the keystone of a problem is right under your nose, but you didn't notice how important that particular factor was.

THE CONSUMER TECH ROOT CAUSE

When Consumer Tech's management team analyzed their *disagreement on how to proceed with the new product,* they found many contributing factors. Ultimately it was traced to the Board of Directors and some overly-optimistic preliminary reports about the successful test results of the new toothbrush. The Board was wildly excited about the potential effect on the stock price if the product would hit the market ahead of the competition.

This explained the source of the underlying pressure to introduce the new toothbrush immediately. But the Board didn't have the whole story. Several quality and inventory issues remained unresolved. So the root cause was defined as:

> *an incomplete briefing of the Board regarding*
> *the Electronic Toothbrush.*

How did this happen? Some enthusiastic staff members passed initial glowing reports to the Board. This is no crime in an open shop. It is natural to want to spread good news to higher ups. No one is to blame for the root cause. That's not the point. The purpose of Problem-Cause Analysis is to learn what happened so successful corrective action can be taken.

Note how different this root cause is from unilateral pressures to resolve the problem. These forces contributed to why the problem existed and partially explained why it persisted. But they weren't enough. That's the power of the root cause. You find a missing explanation that everyone can get behind and you finally have a chance for a lasting fix.

Unfortunately just handling the root cause—giving the Board the whole story now—won't solve the entire problem. But until they have been briefed completely, no problem resolution is likely.

DISTINGUISHING CAUSE FROM EFFECT

During Step 3 you analyze the data you have collected or need to research. Then you look for cause/effect relationships until you find the most fundamental underlying cause. You keep turning over stones and looking underneath until there's nothing left to discover.

Sometimes distinguishing cause from effect is tricky. The dictionary defines a **cause as "anything which produces an effect" and an effect as "that which is produced by a cause."** Big help, right? It helps to think of **causes** as forces that create or worsen problem symptoms, and **effects** as the consequences resulting from causes. But when you're lost between the top and bottom of an iceberg, cause and effect can be confusing.

Try out the *Cause-Effect Analysis Exercise* on the facing page to assess and sharpen your skills. This situation analyzes the dilemma of a computer programmer in the Engineering Department of Consumer Tech who is leading the development of a new application. The lead programmer refused to accept the results of the code review. This is a meeting in which a program is gone over with a fine tooth comb to see if it will do what's intended. Can you tell cause from effect?

CAUSE-EFFECT ANALYSIS EXERCISE

LABEL: Lead programmer disagrees with results of recent code review.

DIRECTIONS: Classify the following factors as either CAUSE (C) or EFFECT (E). Check the answers at the bottom of the page to see if you labeled the factors correctly.

Factor	Cause (C) or Effect (E)
1. Heated words recently between programmers.	_____
2. Different programming methods used prior to review.	_____
3. Programmer frustrated since new programming methods introduced.	_____
4. No training in new methods.	_____
5. Lack of supervision by lead programmer.	_____
6. Name calling during code review.	_____
7. Lead programmer given ''do it your own way'' authority.	_____
8. Old database design selected.	_____
9. 280 hours to fix bugs found in code review.	_____
10. No one enjoys working with lead programmer.	_____
11. Extra staff added as result of poor progress.	_____
12. Lead programmer displayed ''know-it-all'' attitude.	_____
13. Little user input considered in design of new code.	_____

ANSWERS: The following factors were causes: 2, 4, 5, 7, 8, 12 and 13. The remaining factors were effects.

HOW TO FIND THE ROOT CAUSE

By this point in our PS/DM Outline, you have identified quite a few causes. If you've documented Steps 1 and 2 for your *Personal Case Problem,* you need to review the facts, symptoms, proposed labels, and key word definitions, searching for contributing forces. Transfer the causes you've already identified to the *Cause Analysis Worksheet.* This can be a major time saver, but requires the ability to tell causes from effects. If you can't distinguish between cause and effect you'll end up transferring too many items.

CAUSE ANALYSIS WORKSHEET

Statement of the problem

Possible causes

Root cause

SIX TECHNIQUES TO IDENTIFY PROBLEM CAUSES

Problem-Cause Analysis is probably the most demanding action of the entire PS/DM outline.

The six techniques listed below can help. Each will be reviewed individually.

Technique 1. **Brainstorming**
Technique 2. **Positive/Negative Forces Analysis**
Technique 3. **Charting Unknowns**
Technique 4. **Chronological Analysis**
Technique 5. **Repetitive Why Analysis**
Technique 6. **Cause/Effect Diagram**

1. BRAINSTORMING

You can add to your list of potential root causes with brainstorming. Possible questions to use as your focal point are:

"What caused the problem?"
"Why does the problem exist?"
"Where did it start and where did it come from?"
"Why doesn't it resolve itself or just go away?"
"What caused it in the first place?"
"What changed right before things got messed up?"
"Why do you keep getting sucked back into the situation?"
"Why won't things improve no matter what?"

2. POSITIVE/NEGATIVE FORCES ANALYSIS

The now familiar two column worksheet, *Positive/Negative Forces Analysis For Causes,* can be used to stimulate thinking to add to the list of causes. By going back and forth from what minimizes the trouble to what makes it worse, new contributing forces come up that didn't occur to anyone before.

POSITIVE/NEGATIVE FORCES ANALYSIS FOR CAUSES

What forces lessen or minimize the problem?	What forces worsen or contribute to the problem?
(Use the above headings to	create your own worksheet.)

SIX TECHNIQUES TO IDENTIFY PROBLEM CAUSES (Continued)

3. CHARTING UNKNOWNS

Sometimes problem-solving and decision-making groups run dry before they really look comprehensively at the issue. To break through these blind spots, use the *Charting Unknowns Worksheet* to energize creative thinking. In a sense, this is just another brainstorming question but applied with reverse psychology. Mental blocks may develop from focusing too hard on what you do know about the problem. By asking *"What don't we know about the problem?"* hidden facts emerge or new research directions are suggested.

CHARTING UNKNOWNS WORKSHEET

Statement of the problem
What is not known about the problem? (Use the above headings to create your own worksheet.)

4. CHRONOLOGICAL ANALYSIS

The layered drawing of the iceberg shows how unsolved problems evolve. A bad decision causes a production problem. A band-aid solution works temporarily, but creates side-effects. Quick fixes are found for these by-products but they don't stick. Months later no one remembers where it all started.

Using the *Chronological Problem Analysis,* it is possible to recall the sequence of events leading up to the snarled-up situation. Starting from present time, list the major symptoms or causes and examine when each started. This type of investigation reveals cause-effect relationships by identifying what happened before the last blow-up. Often you find an intermediate problem was actually caused by an inappropriate solution made earlier.

CHRONOLOGICAL PROBLEM ANALYSIS WORKSHEET

Major symptom/cause	When did it start?	What happened then?
(Use the above headings to create your own worksheet.)		

CHRONOLOGICAL PROBLEM ANALYSIS (Continued)

Using the *Chronological Problem Analysis Worksheet,* the causes from the Consumer Tech programmer's disagreement were listed in chronological order with the most recent cause at the top.

| Lack of supervision of programming team. |
| Lead selected old database design. |
| Different programming methods used prior to review. |
| Little user input considered in design of new code. |
| No training on new methods. |
| Lead programmer given "do it your own way" authority. |
| Lead programmer displayed a "know-it-all" attitude. |

In this particular case it was determined that the lead programmer's attitude was a personality trait that wasn't about to change. The final analysis showed that giving a "know-it-all" *Do It Your Own Way* authority was what really precipitated the continuing troubles. This is not to point the finger in blame. Some decisions look like the most expedient solution at the time, but later breed other trouble. Hindsight is the best teacher, so put your emphasis on **what**, not **who**.

It helps to plot the results of this analysis on a *Problem Timeline.* This sample gives you an idea of how such a chart looks when done. The clear picture may not answer any specific questions itself. But it shows what to ignore and exactly where to look when you're searching for the root cause.

LEAD PROGRAMMER PROBLEM TIMELINE

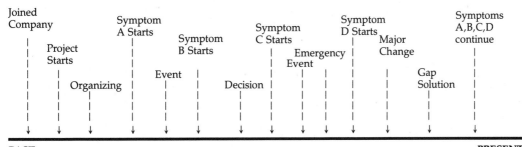

PAST   PRESENT

SIX TECHNIQUES TO IDENTIFY PROBLEM CAUSES (Continued)

5. REPETITIVE WHY ANALYSIS

Extensive analysis sometimes generates many potential causes but no clear *"Aha!"* regarding the root. It helps to trace the evolution of the problem with a **Repetitive Why Analysis.** This procedure distinguishes between the most fundamental causes and their intermediate effects. The logic process used strongly resembles the idea of uncovering a piece of paper which hides another piece of paper, hiding another, etc..

If the root cause doesn't appear during your initial search, find one underlying factor that seems to be most fundamental. Write it in the first box of the *Repetitive Why Worksheet.* Then ask *"What caused that?"* or *"Why is that a problem?"* repetitively until you locate the basic on the chain. An example follows to show how this works.

REPETITIVE WHY WORKSHEET

```
┌─────────────────────────────────────────────────┐
│                                                 │
│                                                 │
│                                                 │
└─────────────────────────────────────────────────┘
```

Which was caused by . . .

```
┌─────────────────────────────────────────────────┐
│                                                 │
│                                                 │
│                                                 │
└─────────────────────────────────────────────────┘
```

Which was caused by . . .

```
┌─────────────────────────────────────────────────┐
│                                                 │
│                                                 │
│                                                 │
└─────────────────────────────────────────────────┘
```

Which was caused by . . .

```
┌─────────────────────────────────────────────────┐
│                                                 │
│                                                 │
│                                                 │
└─────────────────────────────────────────────────┘
```

Which was caused by . . .

```
┌─────────────────────────────────────────────────┐
│                                                 │
│                                                 │
│                                                 │
└─────────────────────────────────────────────────┘
```

REPETITIVE WHY WORKSHEET—SAMPLE

Problem: *Irate customer on the phone*

Fifth time put on hold

Which was caused by...

Inability to get new telephone system to work as designed

Which was caused by...

Incorrect written instructions about process

Which was caused by...

Wrong instruction manual in box with new phone

Which was caused by...

Vacation replacement packers didn't have written policy to follow and inserted wrong manual in product package.

SIX TECHNIQUES TO IDENTIFY PROBLEM CAUSES (Continued)

6. CAUSE/EFFECT DIAGRAM

Another way to logically think Problem-Cause Analysis is to create a *Cause/Effect Diagram.* This is often called a fishbone diagram because its lines resemble that of a discarded skeleton after a good fish dinner. The diagram visually categorizes forces into related groups for simpler analysis.

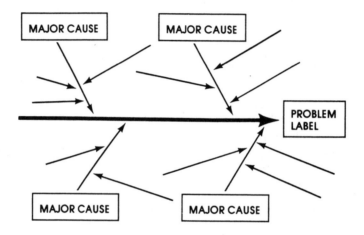

Here is what a Cause/Effect Diagram would look like for Engineering change errors:

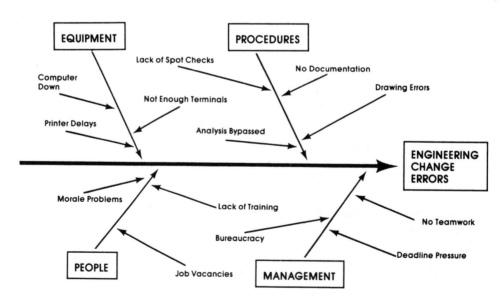

HAVE YOU DONE IT?

Don't move to the solution phase until you are sure you have found the root cause. Test your tentative conclusion using the following *How to Know When You've Found the Root Cause* for verification. To ensure you've analyzed a problem fully and correctly, check the proposed root cause against questions on the checklist. It must pass <u>all</u> of the tests to be the true root cause. If the results of these evaluations aren't conclusive, continue working until the tests are passed. The second phase of the PS/DM Outline will break down without the right root cause.

		HOW TO KNOW WHEN YOU'VE FOUND THE ROOT CAUSE OF A PROBLEM	
		Test Questions	**Yes/No**
Dead End	1.	You ran into a dead end when asking, *"What caused the proposed root cause?"*	_____
Conversation	2.	All conversation has come to a positive end.	_____
Feels Good	3.	Everyone involved feels good, is motivated, and uplifted emotionally.	_____
Agreement	4.	All agree it is the root cause that keeps the problem from resolving.	_____
Explains	5.	The root cause fully explains why the problem exists from all points of view.	_____
Beginnings	6.	The earliest beginnings of the situation have been explored and understood.	_____
Logical	7.	The root cause is logical, makes sense, and dispels all confusion.	_____
Control	8.	The root cause is something you can influence, control, and deal with realistically.	_____
Hope	9.	Finding the root cause has returned hope that something constructive can be done about the situation.	_____
Workable Solution	10.	Suddenly workable solutions, not outrageous demands, that deal with all the symptoms begin to appear.	_____
Stable Resolution	11.	A stable, long-term, once-and-for-all resolution of the situation now appears feasible.	_____

WHEN SHOULD YOU DO WHAT?

Step 3 is the most demanding and confusing step in the PS/DM process. More options are presented here than anywhere else in the PS/DM Outline. This wealth of tools sometimes overwhelms problem-solvers and decision-makers. The *Root-Cause Analysis Program* is a general sequence of techniques which serves as a starting point agenda.

Adjust the order of steps to best approach your situation.

	ROOT-CAUSE ANALYSIS PROGRAM CHECKLIST	Date Completed
Process	1. Agree on which process the group is using at each point in the analysis.	_____
Roles	2. Select an appropriate discussion leader and recorder.	_____
Brainstorm	3. First brainstorm an appropriate question, then document all answers on a simple form such as the **Cause Analysis Worksheet** on page 60.	_____
+ / − Forces	4. Use a *Positive/Negative Forces Analysis* to add to your list of possible causes.	_____
Evaluate	5. Evaluate which cause is most fundamental, and underlying all others.	_____
Diagram	6. Group or categorize the possible causes and determine which category is most basic, using a *Cause/Effect Diagram*.	_____
Repetitive Why	7. Use the *Repetitive Why Worksheet* to trace the most basic cause down to its root. If you hit a dead end, try another starting point down a different path.	_____
Others	8. Use other techniques to add to or evaluate the possible causes on your list until you determine the root cause.	_____
Test	9. When you think you've got it, test your hypothesis using the checklist *How To Know When You've Found the Root Cause of a Problem*.	_____
Persevere	10. If your first hypothesis doesn't prove out, go back and continue your analysis until you succeed. It will be a frustrating waste of time if you skip to solving the problem without an "*Aha!*" experience at this point.	_____

PART VII
STEP 4:
OPTIONAL SOLUTIONS

HOW NOT TO CONSIDER
OPTIONAL SOLUTIONS

STEP 4:
OPTIONAL SOLUTIONS

Finally work can begin on the second phase of the PS/DM Outline, problem-solving. Deciding on a workable solution for the root cause begins with Step 4. This is not a lengthy or complicated step, but is vital in generating agreement on the ultimate decision.

Step 4 is called "Optional Solutions" because the goal is to complete a list of conceivable alternatives. You're looking for any strategies which will address the root cause and resolve the problem once and for all. A complete list of alternatives is essential before proceeding to Step 5.

WHY AS LONG A LIST AS POSSIBLE?

Insisting on a comprehensive list prevents you from rushing off impulsively with the first idea that sounds good. There's a chance that if you follow the first off-the-cuff proposal, it will be inferior, inadequate, or unbalanced. You've come this far by avoiding short-cuts. Don't give in to the temptation now.

Draw on the creative powers of those involved to examine all possible courses of action. This will insure all viewpoints are considered. Though this may not be enough to preclude differences of opinion during decision-making, it at least creates the respect and acceptance so often missing in conflict situations. Everyone may have his or her own hidden agenda and/or pet solution. So be sure to get these in the open and on the list.

Once you get agreement that every course of action is on the list and will be considered, a group will feel some direct ownership in the decision-making process. And this may help to put the group in the mood of generating consensus later.

THE CONSUMER TECH CASE PROBLEM UNFOLDS

Consumer Tech came up with the following list of options (in no particular sequence) to solve the problem of their Electronic Toothbrush:

1. Let the President make the decision and then get the dissenters in line.

2. Replace those who want to introduce the new toothbrush immediately.

3. Start a spin-off operation to produce a model with the new feature.

4. Replace those who want to go more slowly.

5. Threaten to resign to protest pressure from the Board of Directors.

6. Schedule a meeting with the Board to make sure they have the necessary information and let them make the final decision.

7. Develop a joint planning process involving the Board.

8. Let the current thrashing process work itself out...(do nothing).

9. Hire a consultant to mediate the process.

Some of the above are more sensible than others. The "replacement" options, #2 and #4, are downright threatening, but the Consumer Tech management team included them to make the list complete. Once the list is complete, there should be one less thing to argue about, namely: *"Is the best solution on the list?"* If they have done their job, the solution will be on the list.

BUILD A COMPLETE LIST OF OPTIONS
BY ASKING THE RIGHT QUESTIONS

OPTIONAL SOLUTIONS (Continued)

BUILDING A COMPLETE LIST

Following are three techniques to generate a complete list of optional solutions:

> 1. Recovery
>
> 2. Brainstorming
>
> 3. Force-Field Analysis

These techniques are designed to identify strategic directions and basic approaches, not specific tasks. To list every helpful action would make the task monumental. Apply a "seeing the forest, not the trees" concept. If you come up with a large number of action tasks instead of strategies, save them for action planning at Step 6.

TECHNIQUE 1. RECOVERY:

The obvious starting place is to review your notes. The temptation to get rid of symptoms during Problem Analysis is great. You will probably have many possible solutions in your notes from Steps 1, 2, and 3. If so, you have a head start on Step 4. Here is an example of how careful documentation and thorough analysis pays off.

Recover any potential solution strategies discovered earlier and transfer them to the *Optional Solutions Worksheet* on the facing page. These may have been ideas on how to resolve the situation, or they may represent actual past attempts to deal with the problem. Since the motto is *"anything goes"*, previous attempts need to be on the list. An earlier flop may work if better focused. Or old ideas may suggest more workable variations.

OPTIONAL SOLUTIONS (Continued)

OPTIONAL SOLUTIONS WORKSHEET

Root cause to solve	
List all strategies that have any chance of working	Evaluation (Step 5)*

(Leave the Evaluation Column blank until Step 5.)

OPTIONAL SOLUTIONS (Continued)

TECHNIQUE 2: BRAINSTORMING:

Brainstorming seems to have been made for Step 4. Focus your mind on conceiving any strategies that have the slightest chance of resolving the root cause. Consider incredible proposals, ridiculous or unacceptable approaches, all "far-out" suggestions, and anything pertaining to the resolution of the underlying issue.

Research on meetings shows that conservative groups are much less effective in problem resolution than those willing to consider wild-eyed schemes. Removing blinders and internal barriers may generate some crazy ideas. Typically even harebrained proposals can often be molded into workable paths no one would have dreamed of without unrestrained brainstorming. And that's fun too!

Add to your *Optional Solutions Worksheet* as things progress. Be sure to follow the rules of brainstorming and avoid editing or evaluating until the list is complete. Always include *doing nothing* as one option since this course of action should be consciously considered.

Possible target questions to serve as the focal point for this process are:

"What would solve the problem?"

"What strategy could resolve the root cause?"

"What solutions have already been thought of?"

"What approaches haven't been thought of?"

"How could we stop this situation from recurring?"

"What different methods might work?"

"What crazy ideas might help?"

OPTIONAL SOLUTIONS (Continued)

TECHNIQUE 3. FORCE-FIELD ANALYSIS:

The *Positive/Negative Analysis For Solutions* can stimulate thinking just as the force-field format did in the past. Since we're looking for solutions, the two columns play **better** against **worse.** This is similar to the worksheet in Step 3 designed to generate causes. New approaches should be added to the master list of optional solutions.

POSITIVE/NEGATIVE FORCES ANALYSIS
FOR SOLUTIONS

What would make the problem better?	What would make the problem worse?

PART VIII
STEP 5:
DECISION-MAKING

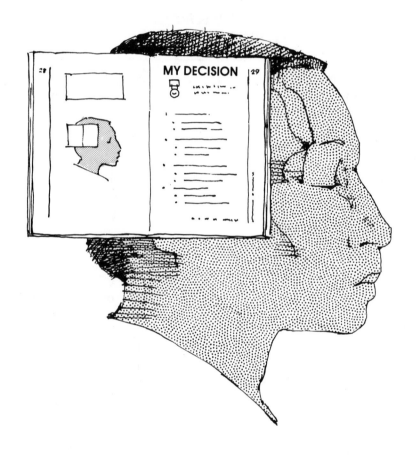

STEP 5: DECISION-MAKING

Decision-Making is the second half of the title of this book. Yet it's taken us a long time to get here. That's because everything up to this point is designed to make decision-making work right.

Step 5 allows you to choose one alternative solution as a course of action. You make a value judgment on what to do about the problem. The result you want is a firm joint decision on the chosen optional solution. This means selecting one strategy from the list in Step 4 that everyone will respect.

Too often decision-making consists of abuse of political power, personal preference, poor leadership, or a macho demonstration of decisiveness. The PS/DM process is designed to avoid these. Having analyzed the problem thoroughly, determined the underlying root cause, and listed possible alternatives allows the problem-solver/decision-maker to make an objective, rational, comparative evaluation.

LINE 'EM UP

The philosophy of Step 5 is **evaluation**—This means lining your ducks up, weeding out the worst choices, and weighing remaining choices against each other. You will consider ranking, prioritizing, and scoring the alternatives to make your choices. The goal is to find the "right" solution using a practical, scientific process.

There are usually several approaches to solving a problem. The team-building/conflict-resolution process built into the PS/DM Outline addresses the choice in the most constructive way. Those involved "own" a portion of the analysis since they participated in its conclusions. Every realistic strategy should be on the list of options. People will continue to have preferences and different points of view. What helps the organization in the long run may hurt an individual or department in the short run. Trade-offs may have to be made. Differing viewpoints always suggest compromise. People may bargain, exchange favors, or apply pressure.

You've worked hard to set things up for an objective comparison, and you're in a good position to pull it off. Remember that the primary concern is to make a firm choice that everybody buys. If they support it, it will work and the implementation that you'll design in Step 6 will be carried out.

A "right" decision may exist, however, it will not work unless those involved "buy-in." A compromise choice may be less risky, and more popular. A secondary workable solution that is agreed-upon is better than a "perfect choice" that continues to create controversy from hidden resistance. So a pragmatic subjective choice is required as well as a "right" objective one. **Once your decision is chosen and agreed to, it is essential to stick with it.**

HOW TO MAKE A DECISION

Following are eight Decision-Making tools. These are presented from the least structured to the most structured:

DECISION-MAKING TOOLS

1. INFORMAL DISCUSSION
2. BRAINSTORMING
3. ELIMINATION
4. WEIGHING AGAINST GOALS
5. WEIGHING AGAINST CONSEQUENCES
6. PRIORITIZING
7. COMBINATION
8. CRITERIA MATRIX

TOOL 1. INFORMAL DISCUSSION:

It is natural to discuss a list of options first. Thinking out loud, bouncing ideas off an interested sounding board, and getting advantages and disadvantages in the open is a healthy starting point for a decision. You can record any conclusions in the evaluation column of the *Optional Solutions Worksheet* from Step 4. This tool is the least structured process for evaluating options, but it plays a critical role in problem-solving and decision-making.

TOOL 2. BRAINSTORMING:

Brainstorming wasn't designed for objective decision-making. The momentum of group think can sway rational analysis away from a balanced evaluation. But it can be an effective method. Possible questions to use as guidelines are:

"How does each alternative solution measure up?"

"Which option seems most workable?"

"Which solution has the best chance to succeed?"

"How risky is each possible solution?"

"Which solution can everyone decide to fully commit to?"

"Which solution do you definitely choose?"

HOW TO MAKE A DECISION (Continued)

TOOL 3. ELIMINATION:

A common occurrence during informal discussion or brainstorming is to discover that some options won't cut it. Eliminating unworkable choices can reduce a long list to something more manageable. You can delete items using specific disqualifying factors such as cost, risk, or time. The following tools may be difficult with an unwieldy list.

Put an "X" next to the options you would eliminate from the list Consumer Tech generated. Then check the answers with those in the upside down box below to see which options Consumer Tech eliminated.

1. Let the President decide and get the dissenters in line _____
2. Replace those who want to introduce the hands-free option now _____
3. Start a spin-off to produce a model with the new feature _____
4. Replace those who want to go slowly _____
5. Threaten to quit in protest of Board pressure _____
6. Fully brief the Board and let them decide _____
7. Develop a joint planning process involving the Board _____
8. Let the current thrashing process work itself out (do nothing) _____
9. Hire a consultant to mediate the process _____

ANSWERS: During the decision-making process, Consumer Tech quickly ruled #2, #4, and #5 as clearly undesirable.

TOOL 4. WEIGHING AGAINST GOALS:

Review your list of remaining options and weigh them against the goals of the organization, department, or personal performance plan. For this to be successful, an accurate, up-to-date strategic plan is required. Problem-solving and decision-making groups often find it necessary to develop or refine organizational or personal goals at this point.

A useful approach to TOOL 4 is to first develop a statement of an ideal situation. How you would want things to be if you had total control over circumstances? Then evaluate your alternative solutions against this scenario.

HOW TO MAKE A DECISION (Continued)

TOOL 5. WEIGHING AGAINST CONSEQUENCES:

You can weigh the potential ramifications of each option using the *Consequences Worksheet* below. List optional solutions in the left column and then predict the likely consequences in the columns to the right. By comparing the contents of one column against the next, you create a risk/reward and cost/benefit analysis. In the *conclusions* column, decide whether the possible benefits and rewards justify the potential costs and risks.

CONSEQUENCES WORKSHEET

Optional Solution	Potential Costs	Potential Risks	Possible Benefits	Possible Rewards	Conclusions

HOW TO MAKE A DECISION (Continued)

TOOL 6. PRIORITIZING:

The *Prioritizing Methods Checklist* on the next page offers six approaches to selecting the best solution from a list. Each method has strengths. Determine which method you think will work best and apply it to your list of options.

A second method you may not be familiar with is, *"bubble-up/bubble-down."* It functions like a computer sorting device. In a forced-pair comparison, you take the first two items on the list and decide which is better. If the second wins, it moves to the top of the list. Otherwise leave them as is and move to the next distinct pair. As an example let's use the remaining items in the Consumer Tech list.

1. Let the President decide and get the dissenters in line
3. Start a spin-off to produce a model with the new feature
6. Fully brief the Board and let them decide
7. Develop a joint planning process involving the Board
8. Let the current thrashing process work itself out (do nothing)
9. Hire a consultant to mediate the process

(#1 and #3 seem to be in the right order, so leave them as is.)

When we compare #3 and #6, the "spin-off" option seems less desirable and should move down.

1. Let the President decide and get the dissenters in line
6. Fully brief the Board and let them decide
3. Start a spin-off to produce a model with the new feature
7. Develop a joint planning process involving the Board
8. Let the current thrashing process work itself out (do nothing)
9. Hire a consultant to mediate the process

This process should continue for all items on the list. A forced-pair prioritizing comparison is finished when there is agreement on the relative position of every item on the list in relation to every other item.

Do you agree with the final order below from the Consumer Tech case or would you organize them differently?

7. Develop a joint planning process involving the Board
6. Fully brief the Board and let them decide
9. Hire a consultant to mediate the process
1. Let the President decide and get the dissenters in line
3. Start a spin-off to produce a model with the new feature
8. Let the current thrashing process work itself out (do nothing)

DECISION-MAKING PRIORITIZING METHODS CHECKLIST

1. Ranking in order of: _____

    Best _____

    Most workable _____

    Reliability _____

    Most tested and proven _____

    Least risky _____

    Staff ability to make it work _____

    Chance for success _____

2. Use forced-pair comparison to *''bubble-up/bubble-down''* items resulting in a prioritized list. _____

3. Get individuals in a group to rate each item and then tabulate ratings using a scale such as: _____

    5 = Top Preference

    4 = High Preference

    3 = OK

    2 = Maybe

    1 = Slim Chance

    0 = No Way

4. Vote where majority rules. _____

5. Prioritize by gut feel, intuition, or comfort zone. _____

6. Compromise. _____

HOW TO MAKE YOUR DECISION
(Continued)

TOOL 7. COMBINATION:

At some point during evaluation, problem-solvers and decision-makers may find that two or more items on the list do not conflict. Solutions that complement each other could work well together. A useful decision-making technique is to categorize remaining options. By combining solutions within a category, it is possible to shorten the list for your final choice. Pool creative thinking on each alternative within a category for more workable outcomes. Decision-making then boils down to a more simple job of comparing categories.

The top three options on the Consumer Tech list aren't mutually exclusive. In fact, all have benefits. After some consideration, the management team decided to combine items #7, #6 and #9. Their list now reads like this:

> 7/6/9. Hire a consultant mediator, fully brief the Board and develop a joint planning process with the Board.
>
> 1. Let the President decide and get the dissenters in line.
>
> 3. Start a spin-off to produce a model with the new feature.
>
> 8. Let the current thrashing process work itself out . . . (do nothing).

SIMPLIFIED DECISION-MAKING

HOW TO MAKE A DECISION
(Continued)

TOOL 8. CRITERIA MATRIX:

A helpful method to visualize decision choices is a *Criteria Matrix.* This is a chart with alternative solutions listed in the left column and the criteria to measure them across the top.

To use the Criteria Matrix, you first must develop a thoughtful *Standards and Criteria List.* Criteria are accepted standards, common sense benchmarks, or proven yardsticks that indicate what an effective solution would look like. List measurement indicators that tell whether a proposed solution is good, bad, or marginal.

You may wish to consider what organizational goals, departmental objectives, and job targets are impacted by the problem. Do validated quality or quantity standards exist? Take into account any time, cost, material, or human constraints or limitations that need to be considered. What negative consequences should your choice avoid at all costs? Look for benchmarks against which to judge the workability of the items on your list of alternative solutions.

Consumer Tech's Management group developed the following list of criteria.

STANDARDS AND CRITERIA LIST

By what standards and criteria should you judge your optional strategies?

Effect on stock price

Expansion of market

Cost-effectiveness

Effect on management and staff morale

Level of risk

CRITERIA MATRIX (Continued)

The alternative solutions are listed in the left hand column of the matrix, with the criteria listed across the top. It is important to use a key word or phrase. If you use lengthy statements or numbers, the matrix won't visually communicate what you're evaluating.

You can rate options using a **+, −, ?** scale, an **A, B, C** label, or a numeric scale of **1 to 3** or **1 to 10.** When using the numeric scale, add up each row to generate a numeric score for each alternative. A weighted evaluation can also be used to give a different multiplier to scores under each criteria. With or without weighting the final ranking comes from adding the ratings in each row. The matrix is helpful in compartmentalizing a complex analysis. But, the answer is no more accurate than the individual scores. Other methods of rating may be more appropriate in specific cases. Be sure to define your scale in the box at the top of the matrix before you begin.

CRITERIA MATRIX

Rating scale:

Alternative Solutions	Evaluation Criteria					RATING

In the resulting boxes, you rate each option against each criteria. We'll see how Consumer Tech rated their alternative solutions on the next page.

CRITERIA MATRIX (Continued)

Consumer Tech chose a 5 point scale. Based on your knowledge of the case, rate the options and add up the scores as you see it. Then compare your ratings with those of Consumer Tech which appear on the following page.

CONSUMER TECH CRITERIA MATRIX

Rating scale:

1 to 5, with 5 = best

Alternative Solutions	Evaluation Criteria					RATING
	STOCK	MARKET	COST	MORALE	RISK	
7/6/9. Consultant mediator/Board briefing/joint planning process						
1. President decides and gets dissenters in line						
3. Start a spin-off to produce a model with the new feature						
8. Let the current thrashing process work itself out. . . . (do nothing)						

THE CONSUMER TECH RANKING

Here's how Consumer Tech scored their remaining options:

Alternative Solutions	Evaluation Criteria					RATING
	STOCK	MARKET	COST	MORALE	RISK	
7/6/9. Consultant mediator/Board briefing/joint planning process	5	5	4	5	5	24
1. President decides and gets dissenters in line	2	3	5	3	3	16
3. Start a spin-off to produce a model with the new feature	4	5	1	4	1	15
8. Let the current thrashing process work itself out (do nothing)	1	3	5	1	1	11

In this case, the bubble-up/bubble-down process yielded the same result as a Criteria Matrix. This is a good double check. In real life you probably wouldn't apply every decision-making tool. Some will be more appropriate than others. Use your judgment.

The final score for each alternative is only as reliable as the accuracy of each individual rating. This process only breaks down a complex evaluation into a series of smaller judgments. So if the top scores are close, don't make your final decision solely by the results of matrix.

BEFORE MOVING ON

Evaluate your final choice with a *Decision Test.* This is done by designing questions to test the workability of your key solution. When evaluating a decision, the form below will determine whether you've picked the ideal decision, the most likely to succeed decision, or the most workable decision. The ideal decision will pass all tests, but may not be workable. In decision-making, perfection is secondary to workability.

DECISION TEST

Test Question	Yes/No/?
1. Does it solve the problem and the root cause?	_____
2. Does it satisfy all established criteria?	_____
3. Does it satisfy all people involved and affected?	_____
4. Can workable action plans be developed to implement it?	_____
5. Is there time to implement it?	_____
6. Do the personnel and resources exist to make it work?	_____
7. Will its implementation end the recurrence of the problem?	_____
8. Have all its risks, disadvantages, and possible consequences been considered?	_____
9. Is it the best choice in terms of:	
a. Benefits	_____
b. Costs	_____
c. Risks	_____
d. Commitment	_____
e. Workability	_____

PART IX
STEP 6:
ACTION PLANNING

*AVOID A "DATA DUMP" WHEN
DESCRIBING YOUR ACTION PLAN*

STEP 6: ACTION PLANNING

The best solution ever conceived and agreed-upon won't solve a problem if it isn't put into action. An action plan details who will do what, by when. An action plan organizes tasks which implement the decision in the real world. Timing, personnel and other resources must be considered and choreographed into action. Setting performance standards, production and quality targets, plus a follow-up monitoring mechanism, is vital to ensure that the plan is carried through.

MURPHY'S LAW

Always consider Murphy's Law; *"That which can go wrong, will."* No matter how well you predict the future, think through the sequence of implementation, or estimate time and resources, your plan will rarely go as conceived. It is better to anticipate problems and prepare as best you can. The best action plans include contingency thinking to avoid Murphy's worst effects.

IS IT WORTH THE TROUBLE?

New managers often ask, *"Why bother to plan at all?"* The answer is simple: you will be much better prepared to adapt and respond even when things go wrong with a plan. Action planning allows for fast adjustment and wise reaction, not a rigid inflexible pattern for the future.

THE VALUE OF PLANNING

THE VALUE OF ACTION PLANNING

Benefits are included in *The Value of Action Planning Checklist* below. Check those items which would help you implement decisions and solutions.

			AGREE
Realistic Actions	1.	They translate decisions into workable realistic actions staff can identify with.	☐
Concrete Programs	2.	They nail down abstract ideas into concrete programs which are achievable.	☐
Specific Assignments	3.	They give specific assignments so individuals know what to do and when.	☐
Clear Expectations	4.	They create clear expectations so staff know how they will be evaluated.	☐
Effective Delegation	5.	They divide responsibility for effective delegation in a simple way.	☐
Mutual Commitment	6.	They build agreement by establishing mutual commitment to the plan.	☐
Coordinate Action	7.	They coordinate action and thus contribute to team-building and teamwork.	☐
Effective Follow-Up	8.	They provide an effective follow-up mechanism by mapping future checkpoints.	☐
Objective Measurement	9.	They establish a basis for objective results measurement.	☐
Clearcut Accountability	10.	They contribute to clearcut accountability by identifying who is responsible for what.	☐
Save Time	11.	They save time by coordinating action and translating decisions into assignments.	☐
Support Workers	12.	They guide management to know how to support workers without over-supervising.	☐
Employee Involvement	13.	They provide good opportunity for employee involvement in the planning process itself.	☐
Insure Results	14.	They ensure results by focusing all resources in the best possible way.	☐

CONSUMER TECH ACTION PLAN

Here's what an initial sketch of the Consumer Tech action plan looked like:

Overall Plan:	Fully brief the Board, develop a joint planning process, using a consultant to mediate the process				
Action	**Responsible Person**				
1. Identify outside consultant	President				
2. Investigate problems in manufacturing	Mfg Mgr				
3. Estimate when quality will become reliable	Qual Mgr				
4. Predict how long current inventory will last	Finance Mgr				
5. New feature introduction marketing plan	Marketing Mgr				
6. Brief consultant	President				
7. Fully brief the Board	President				
8. Set up joint planning process	Consultant				
9. Begin joint planning	Consultant				
10. Develop action plan for implementation	President				

An action plan creates a practical program to translate the decision or overall target into reality. This should resolve the problem and its side effects. The end result of Step 6 is a complete step-by-step road map of how to implement the decision.

ACTION PLANNING TOOLS

The following seven tools should help problem-solvers and decision-makers generate a workable road map to implement their decisions. Each will be briefly considered. The tools are:

1. Recovery
2. Brainstorming
3. Question and Answer
4. Organize

5. Monitoring
6. Resource Estimation
7. Contingency Planning

ACTION PLANNING TOOLS

TOOL 1. RECOVERY:

You probably have a number of action items in your notes from previous steps.
Don't waste these thoughts. After deleting those focused on other root causes or
decision strategies, others should be valuable enough to transfer. Record any
workable ideas on to the *Action Item Worksheet.*

ACTION ITEM WORKSHEET

TOOL 2. BRAINSTORMING:

Continue your creative thinking by brainstorming on the *Action Item Worksheet.*
Questions which will serve as your target are:

"What needs to be done to make this solution work?"

"Who should do what?"

"How do we get from here to there?"

"What is the most efficient budget and schedule?"

"How will we know if we're on or off track?"

"How will we follow up to insure completion?"

ACTION PLANNING TOOLS
(Continued)

TOOL 3. QUESTION AND ANSWER:

Use the *Action Planning Question Checklist* to add to your list. Go through the questions one by one and when you feel each has been thoroughly answered, check it off and move on to the next one. This comprehensive approach will help insure that all bases are covered.

ACTION PLANNING QUESTION CHECKLIST

1. What is the overall objective and ideal situation? _____

2. What is needed in order to get there from here? _____

3. What actions need to be done? _____

4. Who will be responsible for each action? _____

5. How long will each step take and when should it be done? _____

6. What is the best sequence of actions? _____

7. How can we be sure that earlier steps will be done in time for later steps which depend on them? _____

8. What training is required to insure that all staff have sufficient know-how to execute each step in the plan? _____

9. What standards do you want to set? _____

10. What level of volume or quality is desirable? _____

11. What resources are needed and how will we get them? _____

12. How will we measure results? _____

13. How will we follow up each step and who will do it? _____

14. What checkpoints and milestones should be established? _____

15. What are the make/break vital steps and how can we insure that they succeed? _____

16. What could go wrong and how will we get around it? _____

17. Who will this plan affect and how will it affect them? _____

18. How can the plan be adjusted without jeopardizing its results to insure the best response and impact? _____

19. How will we communicate the plan to insure support? _____

20. What response to change and other human factors are anticipated and how will they be overcome? _____

ACTION PLANNING TOOLS
(Continued)

TOOL 4. ORGANIZE:

Use the *Action Plan Form* to put all your proposed actions together in an orderly fashion. The *Overall Target* box should first be filled in with the solution strategy you're trying to implement (chosen in Step 5.) Then, arrange the specific tasks from the *Action Item Worksheet* in sequence in the *Action* column. Next, consider the staff available and assign who will be responsible for what on the form. Define what level of volume or quality must be achieved in the Performance Standard column. Individual training and development is too often forgotten in Step 6. Be sure to include who needs to learn what to make the plan work.

ACTION PLAN FORM

Date:

Overall Target:					
Action	Responsible Person	Performance Standard	Monitoring Technique	Completion Deadline	Resources Needed
1.					
2.					
3.					
4.					
5.					
6.					
7.					
8.					
9.					
10.					
11.					
12.					
13.					
14.					

ACTION PLANNING TOOLS (CONTINUED)

TOOL 5. MONITORING:

The next column to complete on the **Action Plan Form** is for Monitoring Techniques. When you establish a performance standard you determine how well each function must be done. Measurable quotas, targets, goals, or objectives provide a head start on establishing a monitoring system to track the plan's implementation.

Timing is another essential element of the monitoring process. Each item needs a firm *Completion Deadline*. Long or complex activities may benefit from one or several intermediate checkpoints as well.

Things never go exactly as planned. You need to establish a communication and follow-up system so that everyone involved stays informed and keeps the project on track. How will you check back with assigned staff, compare performance to the expected standards, and follow-up to see that assignments will be completed on time?

The **Monitoring Techniques Checklist** suggests methods which can be used for each action item. Select the most appropriate, accurate, easiest, and reliable method which will show both manager and performer how well things are progressing. The best monitoring is self-administered, while the boss and team are watching.

MONITORING TECHNIQUES

1. Production count statistics _____
2. Quality control spot checks _____
3. Work sampling by management _____
4. Personal inspection of all work _____
5. MBWA (management by walking around) _____
6. Checkpoints on action plan _____
7. Reflective indicator statistics (measuring indirect consequences) _____
8. Trend analysis (typically using graphs) _____
9. Compliance reports _____
10. Regular activity reports _____
11. Tickler file _____
12. One-on-one review meetings _____
13. Group staff meetings _____
14. Climate/attitude surveys and written questionnaires _____
15. Customer/user interviews _____
16. Checklist evaluation/audit _____
17. Fitness report essay (comparing actual to ideal) _____
18. Walk through/role play/dummy run procedure _____
19. Budget controls _____
20. Grapevine _____
21. Gut feel _____

ACTION PLANNING TOOLS
(Continued)

TOOL 6. RESOURCE ESTIMATION:

Time is a limited and easily expendable resource, especially without careful action planning, though dollars are watched even more closely in well-run businesses. This is the best time to calculate logistics, budgets, and other hard resources. Include your estimates in the *Resources Needed* column of the form.

TOOL 7. CONTINGENCY PLANNING:

By this time anyone going to the trouble of developing an action plan will think it's near perfect. But what about a small dose of humility? To avoid human and job sacrifices to Murphy's Law, the best insurance is a little contingency planning. Obstacles to successful implementation can be obvious or hidden. Use the *Contingency Planning Worksheet* to think through what could go wrong, what you can do to avoid it, and if worst comes to worst, how you will get out of the pickle.

CONTINGENCY PLANNING WORKSHEET

What could go wrong?	How could you prevent it from happening?	How will you fix it if it happens?

CONTINGENCY PLANNING
(Continued)

One contingency too often ignored is the all-important human factor. People who weren't involved in the PS/DM Outline analysis may misunderstand the solution. Anticipate where you'll run into resistance to change and again decide how to prevent or combat it. The following chart, *How to Handle Resistance to Change*, should provide some helpful suggestions.

HOW TO HANDLE RESISTANCE TO CHANGE

1. Accept It	People need stability and change unstabilizes. Expect resistance, fear and insecurity to the new and unfamiliar.
2. Empathize	Try to understand the reaction by occupying another's point of view for a moment. If you see the personal and emotional impact change creates, you can handle it better.
3. Know Before You Go	Before you introduce change, find out what you're dealing with. Don't rush into the new until you are an expert on the old and current way of doing things. If necessary, wait until an auspicious time.
4. Analyze The Consequences	Who will it affect? How? What might happen that you haven't considered? Consider all possible eventualities and adjust your proposal to maximize the desirable and minimize the undesirable consequences. (If you can't change what you want to, drop it.)
5. Involve Staff	Ask others for input on the new plan, problems it creates, potential benefits, how to best implement it. By asking, discussing, accepting, and group problem-solving, not only will the staff buy into the change, they'll improve on it and make it more workable.
6. Give Advance Warning	The sooner you announce that change is coming, the better. The longer the lead time, the less the shock, and the easier the emotional and intellectual adjustment.
7. Beat The Grapevine	Manage the *PR* (public relations) of your idea effectively. If the idea leaks and the grapevine precedes your announcement, you've got an extra credibility gap to dig yourself out of.
8. Present It Positively	Sell your idea to everyone affected in a way calculated to appeal broadly, and minimize shock, fear and hostility. Be prepared, composed, and constructive—not *spur-of-the-moment* bullheaded.

9.	**Vent Resistance**	Sometimes people just need to ventilate the emotional shock of the unexpected and untried without any response from the boss. Letting them blow off steam in a group planning session or even one-on-one first can clear the air for rational thought.
10.	**Stress Benefits**	Initially emphasize the needs and problems of others and how the change will help them, not you. If it's for them, it's more likely to be viewed as desirable and worth the trouble. You can even offer appropriate rewards for swift, smooth cooperation.
11.	**Explain The Purpose**	If people can see why you want to go to all this trouble, maybe they'll join the effort. Ideally, the team will agree, so start your presentation in terms of the organizational problem you want to solve or improvement to accomplish.
12.	**Reassure Them**	An immediate promise from the boss that no one will lose their job, pay, or future will help. Anticipate specific individual fears and assure all that the worst won't happen, confidently and realistically.
13.	**Stress Growth**	Many people want to get ahead. Change creates opportunities. If you reinforce new approaches by highlighting possible chances for advancement and development, you can entice the ambitious ones over to your side.
14.	**Include Training**	In both your plans and announcements, be sure to include enough re-education and on-the-job training to make the transition smooth. People want to do a quality job, so prevent the fear of failure by promising and conducting supportive training.
15.	**Change Gradually**	Don't expect major readjustment overnight. Plan for step-wise change, fast enough to keep the energy up but slow enough so each step can be smoothly and certainly done.
16.	**Recognize Your Supporters**	Each step of the way acknowledge constructive advice and willing cooperation. A sincere and loud *"thank you"* afterwards will do an awful lot for improving the climate for change next time.

A FINAL ACTION PLAN TEST

After constructing an action plan but before giving the go ahead, evaluate it using the *Action Plan Test.* By testing it against the 13 criteria, you'll get a good sense of its relative effectiveness and completeness. The best action planners religiously play devil's advocate with their draft work, and adjust it wherever necessary until it has the highest chance of coming off without a hitch.

ACTION PLAN TEST

Criteria	Rating
Does your Action Plan identify...	**Yes/No**
1. Specific actions	_____
2. Clear responsibilities	_____
3. Realistic deadlines	_____
4. Clear cut targets (performance standards and production quotas)	_____
5. Coordinated sequence of actions	_____
6. A realistic and workable system	_____
7. Checkpoints for routine follow-up	_____
8. Reliable measurement of results	_____
9. Needed personal development	_____
10. Correctly emphasized priorities	_____
11. Feasible contingency plans (for risky actions or things that might go wrong)	_____
12. Agreements workable for all involved	_____
13. A good chance of achieving the ideal scene	_____

PART X
SUMMARY

EVALUATION OF YOUR OBJECTIVES

After working through the problem-solving and decision-making process presented here, evaluate your personal progress. On a scale of 1 to 10 (10 = high) rate how well you've achieved each of the 13 objectives of this system:

Outline 1. Understand the systematic rational problem-solving outline. _____

Techniques 2. Know how to use the various analytical techniques for each phase. _____

Communication 3. Recognize the vital role communication plays at each step. _____

Questions 4. Know what questions to use in order to stimulate communication at each phase. _____

Anatomy 5. Understand the anatomy of problems and why they persist. _____

Prevent Stress 6. Understand how to confront problems to prevent future stress. _____

Cause & Effect 7. Know how to distinguish between problem causes and effects. _____

Label 8. Know how to label a problem to facilitate discussion and analysis. _____

Root Cause 9. Know how to find a problem's root cause. _____

Solutions 10. Know why it's important and how to brainstorm optional solutions. _____

Decisions 11. Know how to evaluate optional solutions to decide on the most workable strategy. _____

Action Plans 12. Understand the importance of action-planning to implement the chosen solution. _____

Application 13. Know how to use the resource materials to apply the system to real-life problems as they occur in the future. _____

PERSONAL SUMMARY

Answer the following questions to wrap things up and set your sights on the future:

List the key points of this book that you found most valuable:

Which of your personal expectations have been achieved:

Now that you know the PS/DM Outline...what parts of the systematic process have you been applying correctly:

What mistakes have you inadvertently been making in dealing with problems and solutions:

What do you plan to do to improve your problem solving and decision-making skills:

How do you plan to apply what you've learned:

NOTES

FOR OTHER FIFTY-MINUTE SELF-STUDY BOOKS
SEE ORDER FORM AT THE BACK OF THE BOOK.

NOTES

FOR OTHER FIFTY-MINUTE SELF-STUDY BOOKS
SEE ORDER FORM AT THE BACK OF THE BOOK.

NOTES

FOR OTHER FIFTY-MINUTE SELF-STUDY BOOKS
SEE ORDER FORM AT THE BACK OF THE BOOK.

NOTES

NOTES

FOR OTHER FIFTY-MINUTE SELF-STUDY BOOKS
SEE ORDER FORM AT THE BACK OF THE BOOK.

NOTES

FOR OTHER FIFTY-MINUTE SELF-STUDY BOOKS
SEE ORDER FORM AT THE BACK OF THE BOOK.

NOTES

FOR OTHER FIFTY-MINUTE SELF-STUDY BOOKS
SEE ORDER FORM AT THE BACK OF THE BOOK.

THE FIFTY-MINUTE SERIES

Quantity	Title	Code #	Price	Amount
	MANAGEMENT TRAINING			
	Self-Managing Teams	000-0	$7.95	
	Delegating For Results	008-6	$7.95	
	Successful Negotiation—Revised	09-2	$7.95	
	Increasing Employee Productivity	010-8	$7.95	
	Personal Performance Contracts—Revised	12-2	$7.95	
	Team Building—Revised	16-5	$7.95	
	Effective Meeting Skills	33-5	$7.95	
	An Honest Day's Work: Motivating Employees To Excel	39-4	$7.95	
	Managing Disagreement Constructively	41-6	$7.95	
	Training Managers To Train	43-2	$7.95	
	Learning To Lead	043-4	$7.95	
	The Fifty-Minute Supervisor—Revised	58-0	$7.95	
	Leadership Skills For Women	62-9	$7.95	
	Systematic Problem Solving & Decision Making	63-7	$7.95	
	Coaching & Counseling	68-8	$7.95	
	Ethics In Business	69-6	$7.95	
	Understanding Organizational Change	71-8	$7.95	
	Project Management	75-0	$7.95	
	Risk Taking	76-9	$7.95	
	Managing Organizational Change	80-7	$7.95	
	Working Together In A Multi-Cultural Organization	85-8	$7.95	
	Selecting And Working With Consultants	87-4	$7.95	
	PERSONNEL MANAGEMENT			
	Your First Thirty Days: A Professional Image in a New Job	003-5	$7.95	
	Office Management: A Guide To Productivity	005-1	$7.95	
	Men and Women: Partners at Work	009-4	$7.95	
	Effective Performance Appraisals—Revised	11-4	$7.95	
	Quality Interviewing—Revised	13-0	$7.95	
	Personal Counseling	14-9	$7.95	
	Attacking Absenteeism	042-6	$7.95	
	New Employee Orientation	46-7	$7.95	
	Professional Excellence For Secretaries	52-1	$7.95	
	Guide To Affirmative Action	54-8	$7.95	
	Writing A Human Resources Manual	70-X	$7.95	
	Winning at Human Relations	86-6	$7.95	
	WELLNESS			
	Mental Fitness	15-7	$7.95	
	Wellness in the Workplace	020-5	$7.95	
	Personal Wellness	021-3	$7.95	

THE FIFTY-MINUTE SERIES (Continued)

Quantity	Title	Code #	Price	Amount
	WELLNESS (CONTINUED)			
	Preventing Job Burnout	23-8	$7.95	
	Job Performance and Chemical Dependency	27-0	$7.95	
	Overcoming Anxiety	029-9	$7.95	
	Productivity at the Workstation	041-8	$7.95	
	COMMUNICATIONS			
	Technical Writing In The Corporate World	004-3	$7.95	
	Giving and Receiving Criticism	023-X	$7.95	
	Effective Presentation Skills	24-6	$7.95	
	Better Business Writing—Revised	25-4	$7.95	
	Business Etiquette And Professionalism	032-9	$7.95	
	The Business Of Listening	34-3	$7.95	
	Writing Fitness	35-1	$7.95	
	The Art Of Communicating	45-9	$7.95	
	Technical Presentation Skills	55-6	$7.95	
	Making Humor Work	61-0	$7.95	
	Visual Aids In Business	77-7	$7.95	
	Speed-Reading In Business	78-5	$7.95	
	Publicity Power	82-3	$7.95	
	Influencing Others	84-X	$7.95	
	SELF-MANAGEMENT			
	Attitude: Your Most Priceless Possession-Revised	011-6	$7.95	
	Personal Time Management	22-X	$7.95	
	Successful Self-Management	26-2	$7.95	
	Balancing Home And Career—Revised	035-3	$7.95	
	Developing Positive Assertiveness	38-6	$7.95	
	The Telephone And Time Management	53-X	$7.95	
	Memory Skills In Business	56-4	$7.95	
	Developing Self-Esteem	66-1	$7.95	
	Creativity In Business	67-X	$7.95	
	Managing Personal Change	74-2	$7.95	
	Stop Procrastinating: Get To Work!	88-2	$7.95	
	CUSTOMER SERVICE/SALES TRAINING			
	Sales Training Basics—Revised	02-5	$7.95	
	Restaurant Server's Guide—Revised	08-4	$7.95	
	Telephone Courtesy And Customer Service	18-1	$7.95	
	Effective Sales Management	031-0	$7.95	
	Professional Selling	42-4	$7.95	
	Customer Satisfaction	57-2	$7.95	
	Telemarketing Basics	60-2	$7.95	
	Calming Upset Customers	65-3	$7.95	
	Quality At Work	72-6	$7.95	
	Managing Quality Customer Service	83-1	$7.95	
	Quality Customer Service—Revised	95-5	$7.95	
	SMALL BUSINESS AND FINANCIAL PLANNING			
	Understanding Financial Statements	022-1	$7.95	
	Marketing Your Consulting Or Professional Services	40-8	$7.95	

THE FIFTY-MINUTE SERIES (Continued)

Quantity	Title	Code #	Price	Amount
	SMALL BUSINESS AND FINANCIAL PLANNING (CONTINUED)			
	Starting Your New Business	44-0	$7.95	
	Personal Financial Fitness—Revised	89-0	$7.95	
	Financial Planning With Employee Benefits	90-4	$7.95	
	BASIC LEARNING SKILLS			
	Returning To Learning: Getting Your G.E.D.	002-7	$7.95	
	Study Skills Strategies—Revised	05-X	$7.95	
	The College Experience	007-8	$7.95	
	Basic Business Math	024-8	$7.95	
	Becoming An Effective Tutor	028-0	$7.95	
	CAREER PLANNING			
	Career Discovery	07-6	$7.95	
	Effective Networking	030-2	$7.95	
	Preparing for Your Interview	033-7	$7.95	
	Plan B: Protecting Your Career	48-3	$7.95	
	I Got the Job!	59-9	$7.95	
	RETIREMENT			
	Personal Financial Fitness—Revised	89-0	$7.95	
	Financial Planning With Employee Benefits	90-4	$7.95	

OTHER CRISP INC. BOOKS

Quantity	Title	Code #	Price	Amount
	Desktop Publishing	001-9	$ 7.95	
	Stepping Up To Supervisor	11-8	$13.95	
	The Unfinished Business Of Living: Helping Aging Parents	19-X	$12.95	
	Managing Performance	23-7	$19.95	
	Be True To Your Future: A Guide To Life Planning	47-5	$13.95	
	Up Your Productivity	49-1	$10.95	
	Comfort Zones: Planning Your Future 2/e	73-4	$13.95	
	Copyediting 2/e	94-7	$18.95	
	Recharge Your Career	027-2	$12.95	
	Practical Time Management	275-4	$13.95	

VIDEO TITLE*

Quantity	Video Title*	Code #	Preview	Purchase	Amount
	Attitude: Your Most Priceless Possession	012-4	$25.00	$395.00	
	Quality Customer Service	013-2	$25.00	$395.00	
	Team Building	014-2	$25.00	$395.00	
	Job Performance & Chemical Dependency	015-9	$25.00	$395.00	
	Better Business Writing	016-7	$25.00	$395.00	
	Comfort Zones	025-6	$25.00	$395.00	
	Creativity in Business	036-1	$25.00	$395.00	
	Motivating at Work	037-X	$25.00	$395.00	
	Calming Upset Customers	040-X	$25.00	$395.00	
	Balancing Home and Career	048-5	$25.00	$395.00	
	Stress and Mental Fitness	049-3	$25.00	$395.00	

(*Note: All tapes are VHS format. Video package includes five books and a Leader's Guide.)

THE FIFTY-MINUTE SERIES
(Continued)

	Amount
Total Books	
Less Discount (5 or more different books 20% sampler)	
Total Videos	
Less Discount (purchase of 3 or more videos earn 20%)	
Shipping ($3.50 per video, $.50 per book)	
California Tax (California residents add 7%)	
TOTAL	

☐ Send volume discount information.

☐ Please charge the following credit card

☐ Please send me a catalog.

☐ Mastercard ☐ VISA ☐ AMEX

Account No. _____ Name (as appears on card) _____

Ship to: _____ Bill to: _____

_____ _____

_____ _____

_____ _____

Phone number: _____ P.O. # _____

All orders except those with a P.O.# must be prepaid.
For more information Call (415) 949-4888 or FAX (415) 949-1610.

BUSINESS REPLY
FIRST CLASS   PERMIT NO. 884   LOS ALTOS, CA

POSTAGE WILL BE PAID BY ADDRESSEE

Crisp Publications, Inc.
95 First Street
Los Altos, CA 94022

NO POSTAGE
NECESSARY
IF MAILED
IN THE
UNITED STATES